Real-World Math Projects for Gifted Learners, Grades 4–5

Helping bring mathematics and engineering to life, these challenging lessons give teachers an exciting tool for engaging advanced learners through creativity and hands-on products. Units are driven by standards and invite students to become baseball field architects, create flying jellyfish, make a gnome hat parachute, scale skyscrapers, and more! Each project includes step-by-step lesson plans with reproducible templates, time estimates, and a materials list. While centered on STEAM (science, technology, engineering, arts, and mathematics) competencies, true to real-world experiences, these hands-on projects span the curriculum—including writing and public speaking—and while they suit entire classrooms and smaller groups, they can also be easily adapted to individual projects for independent study and home school.

Mark Hess is a board member for Supporting the Emotional Needs of the Gifted (SENG) as well as President-Elect of the Colorado Association for Gifted and Talented. With over 33 years teaching gifted learners, Mark is currently the gifted programs specialist in a large, urban district in Colorado Springs.

Real-World Math Projects for Gifted Learners, Grades 4–5

Mark Hess

Routledge
Taylor & Francis Group

NEW YORK AND LONDON

Cover image credit: ©Getty Images

First published 2022
by Routledge
605 Third Avenue, New York, NY 10158

and by Routledge
2 Park Square, Milton Park, Abingdon, Oxon, OX14 4RN

Routledge is an imprint of the Taylor & Francis Group, an informa business

© 2022 Taylor & Francis

The right of Mark Hess to be identified as author of this work has been asserted in accordance with sections 77 and 78 of the Copyright, Designs and Patents Act 1988.

Library of Congress Cataloging-in-Publication Data
Names: Hess, Mark, 1966– author.
Title: Real-world math projects for gifted learners, grades 4–5 / Mark Hess.
Description: New York, NY : Routledge, 2022. | Includes bibliographical references.
Identifiers: LCCN 2021044833 (print) | LCCN 2021044834 (ebook) | ISBN 9781032190938 (hardback) | ISBN 9781032190921 (paperback) | ISBN 9781003257646 (ebook)
Subjects: LCSH: Mathematics—Study and teaching (Elementary) | Project method in teaching. | Gifted children—Education.
Classification: LCC QA135.6 .H475 2022 (print) | LCC QA135.6 (ebook) | DDC 372.7/044—dc23/eng/20211119
LC record available at https://lccn.loc.gov/2021044833
LC ebook record available at https://lccn.loc.gov/2021044834

ISBN: 978-1-032-19093-8 (hbk)
ISBN: 978-1-032-19092-1 (pbk)
ISBN: 978-1-003-25764-6 (ebk)

DOI: 10.4324/9781003257646

Typeset in Palatino, Futuro, and Rockwell
by Apex CoVantage, LLC

■ Contents

Contents

Introduction

I loved math when I was a kid. I loved racing through problem sets in 1970s textbooks, and I always wanted to be the first one done. I remember a time in third grade when I vaulted from my desk and ran with my assignment to the front of the classroom so I could slam it into the in-basket ahead of one of my classmates. I took pride in getting all the problems right and calling out my grade, "Minus zero!" as the teacher called my name. Yep, that's how grades were recorded in those days.

Math was easy. Math was fun. I never studied for a math test. One day in high school, to my dismay, I could not solve a math problem on a test in my precalculus class—could not even finish the test before the end of the 50-minute class period. I got a D. To a gifted kid with perfectionist tendencies, it felt like I'd been punched in the stomach. At the end of that semester, I switched out of precalculus into an advanced writing class. Although my life as an English teacher and author took off from that point, I had lost something very important . . . namely, an opportunity. I had lost the opportunity—academically—to understand what it feels like to struggle and grow.

I call it *surfing the wave of wonderfulness* (www.nagc.org/blog/surfing-wave-wonderfulness). Gifted kids often ride high atop this wave, completing assignments with ease, hardly trying yet living an academic life of praise for being smart and talented. Who wouldn't want to ride that wave? Who wouldn't want to be told how brilliant they were? It feels fantastic when it all comes so effortlessly. That's the problem, though—*effortlessly*. The problem comes when gifted kids fall off the wave. Sometimes gifted children build an identity on not only academic success but also the ease of success. It's not good enough to do well in school, but somehow—oddly—that success must be effortless as well. It can become a gifted learner's identity in those early years of school—not just as a learner but literally who they believe themselves to be. Anything less is a sort of failure, and it's hard to let go of that feeling.

Over the years, I've found mathematically gifted children to be amongst the first to give up when faced with a difficult task, and I believe this behavior is related to the nature of math in the younger grades where there are definite right and wrong answers. When you are wrong, you are *dead* wrong. Accustomed to "getting it" so quickly, it feels unpleasant to struggle. It's supposed to be easy, isn't it? We want our gifted children to grow, however, to fail forward within a challenging yet safe environment. So how do we help mathematically gifted kids become familiar with the icky feeling in one's stomach that signals frustration and struggle? How do we create a safe atmosphere where they can grow without facing the black and white of right and wrong? Where might resilience as a learner blossom?

DOI: 10.4324/9781003257646-1

Real-world, hands-on math and engineering projects are one answer. Through math projects, students find many correct answers and many alternatives and pathways to success. The design aspects of projects invite creativity. The process of creation invites revision. In projects, new math skills and challenges are met in a natural flow of discovery. Instead of grades and percentiles, students and teachers evaluate themselves and each other on rubrics which cite degrees of success and suggested improvements—rubrics where shades of gray replace the black and white of right and wrong.

Simply put, the projects in this book grew out of meeting gifted students' academic and social-emotional needs. During my years as an elementary gifted resource teacher, I was fortunate to have worked with some outstanding teachers who used pretests to guide differentiation in math. When some students tested out of entire units, our plan was that these students would be sent to my classroom for enrichment and further challenge. Students flowed in and out of my classroom—some staying for a couple of days, some remaining on a regular basis for the bulk of an entire school year. Sometimes only three or four students worked with me. Sometimes I taught as many as 20 who had "differentiated out" of a unit. I needed to be as flexible as my colleague back in the regular math classroom. I needed units that could be delivered individually as well as to a group and that could be paused and taken up again at a later time. I needed engaging ideas because I never wanted the math work in my room to feel like more work. At the same time, I hoped to be like a good tour guide at a medieval cathedral. I didn't want to do all the talking but wanted to be able to step aside and let the tourists admire the beauty on their own. These circumstances guided the challenges I wanted to present to my students through real-world math projects.

The projects came from both natural as well as unlikely places. One natural place was right outside our window in Colorado Springs—Pikes Peak. It seemed natural to take advantage of the math applications that could be found scaling that mountain. Grandeur is naturally intriguing—whether it be natural grandeur like Pikes Peak or a manmade grandeur we find in skyscrapers. A skyscraper's scale, design, and engineering hold wonderful mysteries. Why not bring this wonder into a hands-on engineering and math unit called Scaling Skyscrapers?

Some of the units, however, grew out of seemingly random or chance encounters with materials at hand. For years, I had taught units about gliders, and I kept a paper cylinder glider on my desk. One day I challenged a fifth grader to a cylinder glider–throwing contest. Tossing the cylinder around the classroom, we wondered together if a cylinder glider would fly more accurately with a tail attached. We began to experiment. This event happened to coincide with the donation of many paper towel tubes to my craft supplies, and the Jellyfish Flier project was born. In a similar fashion, as my accelerated group of fourth and fifth graders created three-dimensional cones for a geometry lesson, a red cone lying on a desktop looked so much like a garden gnome's hat that I couldn't resist transforming it into the Cones and Gnome Hat Parachutes unit.

We teachers are often guilty of gravitating toward subjects we love. Like many baseball fans, I am swept away by baseball fever in the spring. As school closes each year, I have inserted baseball into the curriculum in different ways—pennants, baseball cards, uniforms. Baseball Field Landscape Architects is one of these units. In contrast at the beginning of the school year, setting up my classroom always gives me time to wonder and brainstorm ways to engage kids. Readying desktops with nametags one year, I thought about how important this simple tag becomes to a student's "place" in my classroom, the pride of ownership that accompanies it, and the familiarity and identity that come with this one little tag. Why not design our own nametags, and why not make it a lesson in economics as well?

No reading student ever asks, "When am I ever going to use this in real life?" Reading and communication are understood as essential components to life and learning, and math and math logic should be too. As teachers, we can easily become focused on advancing the math curriculum, ticking the math standards off our "must-do" list, and preparing for the next assessment without exploring the rich mathematical world around us. The math projects in this collection, however, are designed to both stretch a student's abilities in an engaging, hands-on manner as well as provide a safe atmosphere where there are degrees of right and wrong, levels of success, and a focus on the process rather than on the nuts and bolts of mathematical calculation. I hope your students love them as much as mine have over the years, and I hope you have as much fun teaching them as I have, too.

The Jellyfish Flier

Background

Our jellyfish fliers work really well, and they look just like their namesakes! My students had so much fun with this STEM (science, technology, engineering, mathematics) challenge across the curriculum with an emphasis on math.

This unit will challenge students with math applications in engineering and design tasks—perhaps in ways they have never been challenged before. Not only is the unit an outstanding way to stretch a student's abilities, but it also offers unique cross-curricular tasks.

Success will require your students bring together challenging calculations, geometry, engineering, graphic design, and technical drawing—with a little research and writing thrown in to boot.

Some of your students will readily adapt to these tasks depending upon their skill sets and the development of their executive functioning skills. Let's not forget that gifted learners come in unique and infinite varieties. Although it will be important to lend appropriate support to some students, it will be equally important to allow others to proceed at a quicker pace. One of the advantages of this differentiated approach is that students who are working more quickly will also be producing examples of products for students working at a slower pace.

Preparation Notes

Working through this unit as if you were a student is an excellent (and fun) way to prepare—especially if you are not experienced with drafting and technical drawing. You'll experience some of the same frustrations the students experience and generate many of the same questions in your own mind. Feeling a little frustrated? That's OK too! You will be better prepared to urge the students to work through any feelings of frustrations they have, to be resilient, and not to let perfectionism rule their emotions. The most important lessons in gifted and talented units may be the social and emotional ones. This unit is designed to stretch and challenge students, and this process necessarily requires a bit of discomfort. Those little icky feelings we get inside are how we know we are learning something new and challenging.

DOI: 10.4324/9781003257646-2

Unit Objective

The student will:

◆ Understand ratios and scale and apply them to technical drawing tasks.
◆ Use geometry to solve real-world math problems.
◆ Apply an understanding of surface area to three-dimensional shapes.
◆ Understand ways math can be applied to a real-world design and product development task.

Active Common Core Math Standards

All Common Core State Standards throughout this work are © Copyright 2010 National Governors Association Center for Best Practices and Council of Chief State School Officers. All rights reserved.

CCSS.MATH.CONTENT.6.G.A.1

Find the area of right triangles, other triangles, special quadrilaterals, and polygons by composing into rectangles or decomposing into triangles and other shapes; apply these techniques in the context of solving real-world and mathematical problems.

CCSS.MATH.CONTENT.6.G.A.3

Draw polygons in the coordinate plane given coordinates for the vertices; use coordinates to find the length of a side joining points with the same first coordinate or the same second coordinate. Apply these techniques in the context of solving real-world and mathematical problems.

CCSS.MATH.CONTENT.6.SP.B.4

Display numerical data in plots on a number line, including dot plots, histograms, and box plots.

CCSS.MATH.CONTENT.6.SP.B.5

Summarize numerical data sets in relation to their context, such as by:

CCSS.MATH.CONTENT.6.SP.B.5.A

Reporting the number of observations.

CCSS.MATH.CONTENT.6.SP.B.5.B

Describing the nature of the attribute under investigation, including how it was measured and its units of measurement.

CCSS.MATH.CONTENT.6.SP.B.5.C

Giving quantitative measures of center (median and/or mean) and variability (interquartile range and/or mean absolute deviation), as well as describing any overall pattern and any striking deviations from the overall pattern with reference to the context in which the data were gathered.

CCSS.MATH.CONTENT.6.SP.B.5.D

Relating the choice of measures of center and variability to the shape of the data distribution and the context in which the data were gathered.

CCSS.MATH.CONTENT.6.RP.A.3

Use ratio and rate reasoning to solve real-world and mathematical problems, e.g., by reasoning about tables of equivalent ratios, tape diagrams, double number line diagrams, or equations.

CCSS.MATH.CONTENT.7.G.A.1

Solve problems involving scale drawings of geometric figures, including computing actual lengths and areas from a scale drawing and reproducing a scale drawing at a different scale.

CCSS.MATH.CONTENT.7.G.B.4

Know the formulas for the area and circumference of a circle and use them to solve problems; give an informal derivation of the relationship between the circumference and area of a circle.

CCSS.MATH.CONTENT.7.G.B.6

Solve real-world and mathematical problems involving area, volume and surface area of two- and three-dimensional objects composed of triangles, quadrilaterals, polygons, cubes, and right prisms.

Launch

The Giant Jellyfish Invasion Mystery

Engage the students' natural sense of curiosity with the first section of the "The Giant Jellyfish Invasion Mystery" located online at www.thestar.com/news/world/2013/09/16/the_giant_jellyfish_invasion_mystery.html.

This article is especially good for us because it contains challenging vocabulary for upper elementary, and in a read-aloud, gifted learners will be challenged to synthesize the meaning. Stop and answer questions as they arise.

Read aloud only the first two sections of the article (to the section titled "Ancient creatures"), and project the photos onto a screen if you have that capability. The photos alone are pretty amazing! Allow students to comment freely on what they see and hear, and you may follow up with some of the following critical thinking questions:

- The first paragraph opens, "The gelatinous masses on the deck of the Myoho-maru could charitably be described as the colour of weak tea. They quivered as the boat pitched in the choppy morning waves. The blobs had been pulled in from the sea along with an octopus, a clutch of squid and a thousand frantically flopping finfish, the day's intended catch." What do you think *gelatinous* means? This paragraph is very descriptive. Why do you think the author opens the article in this way? Why is *colour* spelled the way it is? Is this a proofreading error?
- In your own words, describe the mystery concerning the giant jellyfish.
- What does Shin-ichi Uye mean when he says, "Although the jellyfish have no words to speak to humans, they are giving a sign to humans by aggregating themselves grotesquely. We human beings have to learn the message from them"?
- Speculate about what is causing the abundance of jellyfish off the coasts of Japan.
- Does this article make you want to find out more?

Follow-Up

Project onto the screen or share more photos of jellyfish. They are amazing creatures. Invite the students to name other creatures that people find amazing. Why are these other creatures amazing? Dinosaurs, for example, are intriguing to many. Why?

As a transition to the first lesson, explain that companies have taken advantage of amazing, high-interest creatures for years to help sell their products. Cheetos is marketed by a cartoon cheetah. Sinclair Oil's logo includes a dinosaur (why, by the way, is this ironic?). You'll run faster and jump higher in Puma shoes—not in regular "house cat" shoes. Gorilla Glue really does the job unlike, for example, gnat glue. In this math, engineering, and design project, you'll be working for a company that is developing a toy based on the intrigue of jellyfish!

Lesson 1.1 Drafting and Design of the Jellyfish Flyer

In this lesson, students will calculate scale while creating blueprints for the Jellyfish Flyer. Students will use technical drawing skills, knowledge of geometry, and measurement to create accurate drawings.

Materials

- Tape
- Small plastic T-square, one per student (available at discount prices online; see photos that follow)
- 12" × 18" white construction paper, one sheet per student

Estimated Time

1 to 2 hours (perhaps even 3 hours if students do not have experience with T-squares)

Procedure

We begin this lesson with instructions for the design of our jellyfish fliers. Distribute the memo from the Creative Team to the students, and clarify any questions as necessary.

Memo

From: Creative Team

To: Design and Product Development Department

We're eager to develop a new idea. We think it will be a big seller! We're calling it the jellyfish flier. Imagine a tube-like glider slicing through the air, flying 30 feet and more with jellyfish-like tendrils trailing behind. It's made out of a simple cardboard cylinder like a paper-towel tube. This is our new Jellyfish Flier!

Our design and production crew needs blueprints right away.

Submit accurate drawings showing the flier at 2.5:1 scale.

Show the flier in side view, top view, and an artistic perspective drawing.

Our sketch follows.

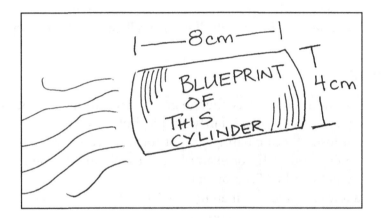

Key Questions for the Product Development Department

- What materials will you need?
- Which tools will you need?
- What calculations will need to be made?
- What skills will you rely on?
- Can you state the request in your own words?
- Who will be useful in a collaboration?

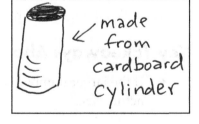

Teacher Notes

I invite students to think about the answers to the questions posed by the Creative Team on their own. Then students may collaborate to add details and find solutions. After a few minutes to collaborate, we come together in a full class discussion to make sure we can proceed successfully.

Blueprints

I have an engineering classroom, and my gifted and talented education (GATE) kids start learning how to use a T-square in third grade. I highly recommend this old-school approach if you haven't discovered the wonderful world of T-squares in a STEAM curriculum. The kids have to pull together measurement and artistic skills to be successful. Some students become very skilled by the end of fifth grade; others are still trying to figure things out. Nonetheless, T-squares are a great way to add logic, grit, and challenge to your curriculum. A few photos follow that show our process.

Alternately, the design and blueprints can be accomplished with a regular ruler and compass if you do not use a T-square, and that in itself is an excellent task if accuracy is required.

Calculations

In my fourth- and fifth-grade math challenge group, few students know what *scale* means, but they catch on quickly. Let's keep it fairly simple, but we want the CONCEPT to stick. In order to circumvent formally calculating proportions, we can simply rely on a gifted kid's mathematical reasoning ability. If, for example, a 2:1 scale means the item is two times the size of actual size, what would 2.5:1 scale mean?

Talk through a few examples . . . if an item is 4:1 scale in a blueprint and actual size is 20 centimeters, what would the scaled blueprint drawing size be (80 centimeters)? If an item is 1:4 scale in a blueprint, and the actual size is 20 centimeters, what would the scaled drawing size be (5 centimeters)? Small toy cars, for example, are often made at 1:64 in scale—quite small in comparison to a real car. Would it be a good idea to try to draw the Eiffel Tower in 2:1 scale? What might be a reasonable scale for a drawing of the Eiffel Tower?

Key Takeaways About Scale

- ◆ If the larger number is first in the ratio, then the drawing shows the item larger than actual size.
- ◆ If the smaller number is first in the ratio, then the drawing shows the item smaller than actual size.

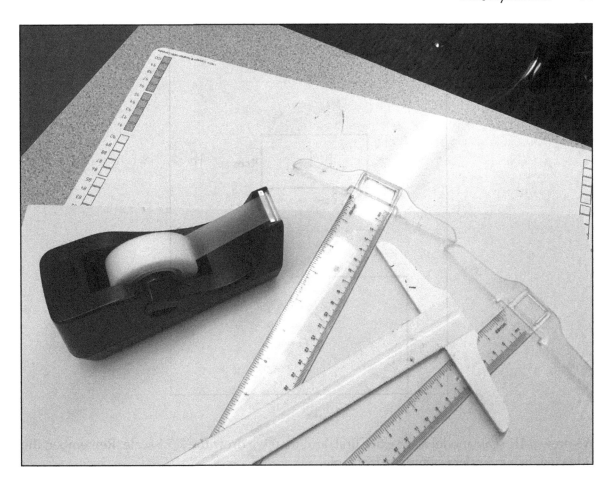

A simple and inexpensive T-square set-up includes tape, construction paper, economy T-squares, and a student whiteboard or edge of a desk as a drafting board.

For basic introductions to technical drawing or drafting, see these videos:

Introduction to Technical Drawing

www.youtube.com/watch?v=YE0oZZO7vbk

Drawing with a T-Square and Set Square

www.youtube.com/watch?v=nA-mCsVLXy8

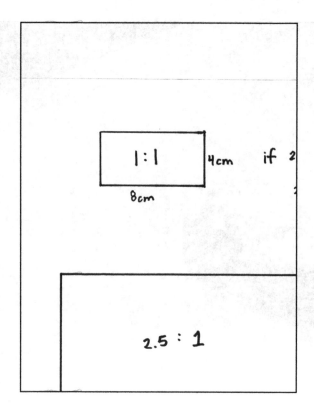

We drew a 1:1 scale model as practice first, and then we drew the 2.5:1 scale. Remember, the side view of a cylinder is simply a rectangle.

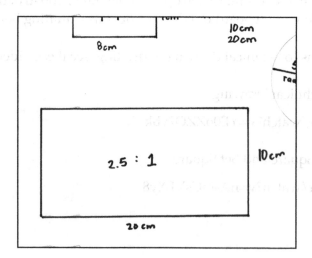

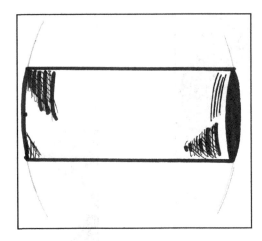

The top view of a cylinder is a circle. It's fun to draw with compasses. Even our fifth graders are inexperienced with a compass, however, so this may take a few tries.

Make sure the students understand—at 2.5:1 scale—that the cylinder's radius is 5 centimeters. The actual diameter of the tube's circular opening is 4 centimeters. At two and a half times the actual size, the diameter of the circular opening is 10 centimeters (4 cm × 2.5 = 10 cm). The radius of a circle with a diameter of 10 centimeters, therefore, is 5 centimeters. See the drawing of the circle in the sample.

You may find it useful to review geometry terms for circles like *radius, diameter, circumference,* and *pi.*

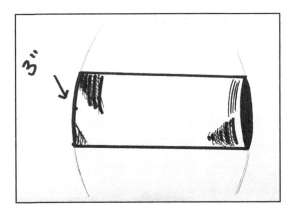

It was fun to play around with some different techniques on the perspective drawing of the cylinder (shown earlier). Skilled drafters will use the compass to make arcs at each end of the tube and use shading techniques to suggest curvature. Kids' artistic talents start to emerge here.

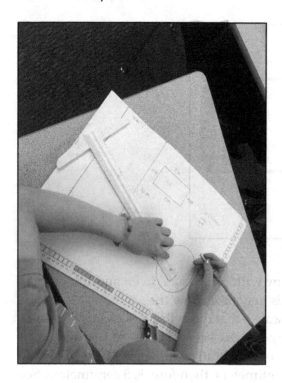 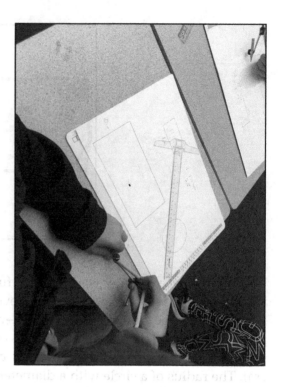

Some kids really take to the process. It's a great way to ferret out different skills. Let's keep in mind that not everyone is good at everything! Here is a chance to talk about social-emotional skills involving resilience and perfectionism.

With blueprints developed, we move on to lesson 1.2, Carded Bubble Packaging.

Lesson 1.2 Carded Bubble Packaging

In lesson 1.2, students will develop designs for the packaging of the Jellyfish Flier product. Playing the role of product design engineers, mathematicians, and graphic artists, our students will calculate accurate measurements for the surface area of the display card and bubble. As graphic designers, students will gather information about jellyfish in order to combine it with artistic designs to make the packaging attractive to collectors.

Materials

◆ Handout: "Memo from Production Management and Marketing Departments"
◆ Markers, colored pencils

Estimated Time

1.5 hours

Procedure

Distribute the memo from the Production Management and Marketing Departments. This memo can be a bit confusing; after all, it's designed to be that way! That's why it helps to break this memo down sentence by sentence, and we need to be careful to figure out the important information and instructions contained within. Discerning readers must have the ability to sort and organize instructions—as with extended math word problems on standardized state-testing tasks.

Using the think–pair–share approach, students first process the memo on their own and then share what they understand with a partner. After, the whole class comes together to clarify understanding.

Memo

From: Production Management and Marketing Departments

To: All Departments

We have decided to market the jellyfish fliers in carded bubbles. You will see the design attached.

We think it would be fantastic if we made these jellyfish fliers into collectibles. The back side of each card will feature different interesting facts about jellyfish. Kids will want to collect all the different cards and designs.

From the RESEARCH DEPARTMENT, we need enough fun information and interesting facts to fill the back side of the card (as seen in the attached).

From the CREATIVITY and GRAPHIC DESIGN DEPARTMENTS, we need the cards to look fantastic! They need to jump off the shelves and grab potential customers! We imagine a colorful card with an eye-catching title on the front. We imagine a colorful backside of the card with the facts and maybe a small illustration.

From the DESIGN and PRODUCT DEVELOPMENT TEAM, our manufacturer needs an accurate measurement of the area of the card. Use the back panel for your calculations, and write the total area of the back side of the card in the margin.

We also need to know the area of the space where the title will be designed. In addition, we need the percentage of the space the title takes up on the front of the card. It looks like the title takes up about 33% of the front of the card, but we need solid numbers here. Every penny counts in the design and printing process!

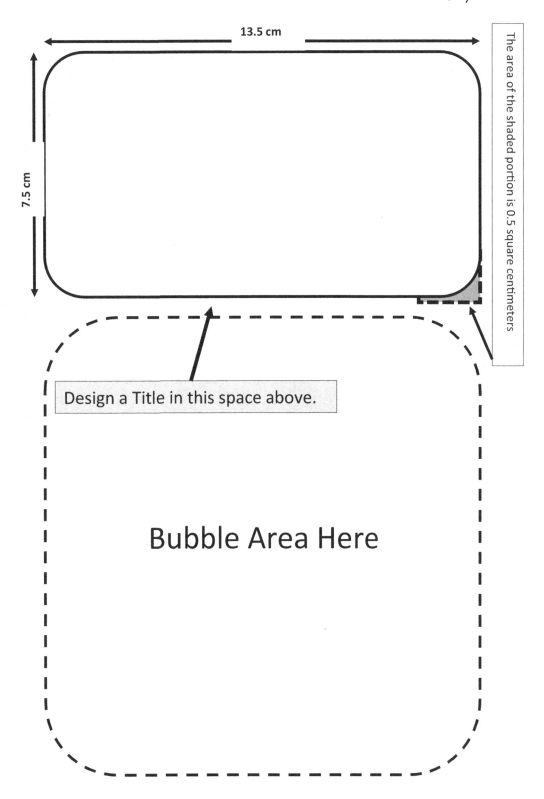

13.5 cm

7.5 cm

The area of the shaded portion is 0.5 square centimeters

Design a Title in this space above.

Bubble Area Here

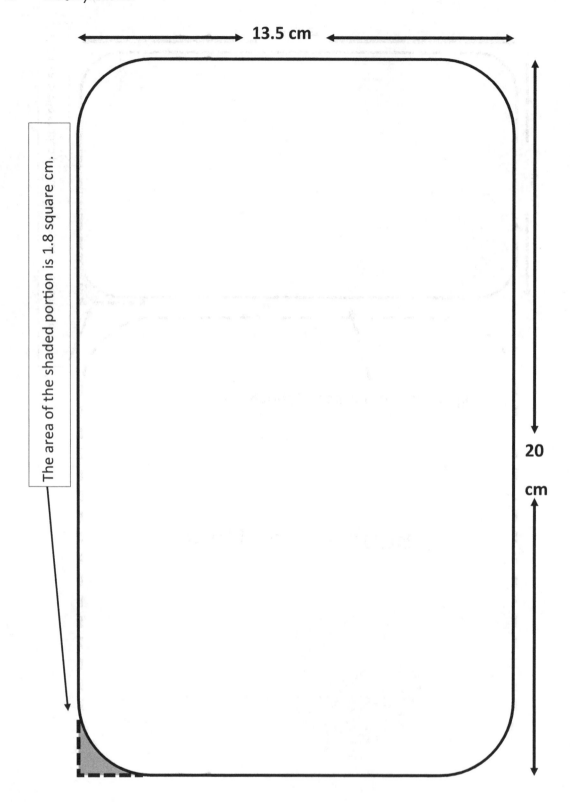

13.5 cm

20 cm

The area of the shaded portion is 1.8 square cm.

Teacher Notes

Samples of student designs are included later.

For the geometry calculations, make sure to use the measurement notes on the sheets themselves. Do not make measurements with a ruler. When these activity sheets are printed, they may print at slightly different sizes . . . so use the measurements stated on the sheets.

I allow the use of calculators for my fourth-grade students and sometimes for fifth graders. These are new concepts for them, and I want them to understand the mathematical logic and process more than anything else. Students gifted in mathematical ability are sometimes phenomenal at calculations—sometimes not. Let's honor both sorts of gifted mathematicians.

Area of Back of Card

To calculate the area of the back, multiple the length by width and subtract out the area of each rounded corner.

Length × Width—20 cm. × 13.5 cm = 270 cm^2

Rounded Corners—1.8 cm^2 × 4 corners = 7.2 cm^2

340 cm^2 − 3.2 cm^2 = 262.8 cm^2 Total Area of Back

Area of Title Space on Front

To calculate the title space area on the front, multiply the length by the width and subtract out the areas of the rounded corners (as earlier).

Length × Width = 13.5 cm × 7.5 cm = 101.25 cm^2

Rounded Corners = 0.5 cm^2 × 4 = 2 cm^2

101.25 cm^2 − 2 cm^2 = 99.25 cm^2

Percentage

We already know the total area of the front of the card from our calculations of the back side's area (336.8 cm^2). We need to divide the area of the title space on the front by the total area of the whole card to find the percentage of the title area for the front of the card.

99.25 cm^2 / 262.8 cm^2 = 37.77% (rounded)

Follow-up question: **Why would the jellyfish flier company need to know these calculations? Why would the calculations need to be accurate?**

Sample responses: The pennies add up in a large manufacturing operation. Larger surface areas mean larger costs for cardboard. Machines must be set to cut shapes accurately and to design standards, and any waste of cardboard is money wasted as well.

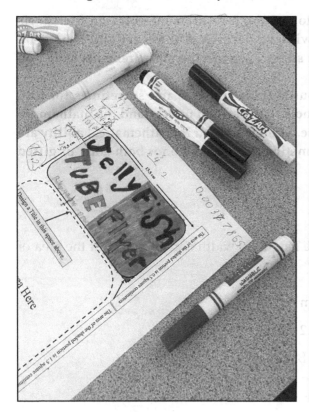

Students will need to gather facts about jellyfish in order to complete the narratives for the back of the carded bubble. Information about various jellyfish—along with spectacular photos—is readily available online.

As students begin to research jellyfish, they will find some pretty amazing photos. This is an excellent opportunity to talk about reliable sources. Is it possible that some of the photos of the most amazing jellyfish are not real? How can we determine the validity of sources?

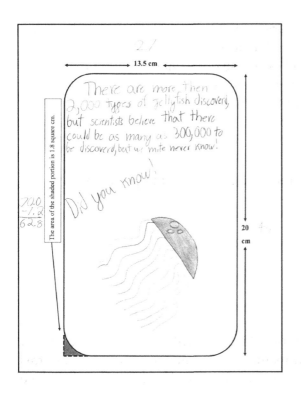

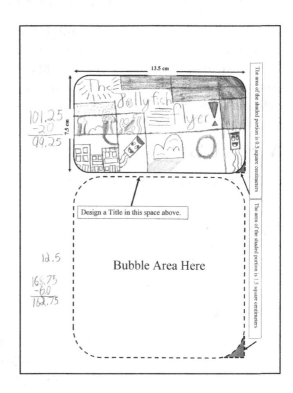

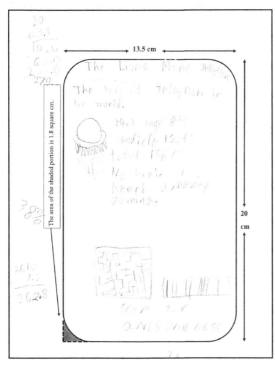

Lesson 1.3 Calculating the Surface Area of a Cylinder and Tube

Our Jellyfish Fliers will soar through the air wrapped with the coolest of cool decals on their sides, but in order to begin making these graphic designs, our manufacturing department will need to know the surface area of the tubes. These decals have to fit! In this lesson, students calculate the surface area of a cylinder and then subtract the circular ends of the cylinder to determine the accurate surface area of the tube flier.

Materials

◆   Handout: "Memo from the Design and Product Development Department"

Estimated Time

20–30 minutes

Procedure

Distribute the memo from the Design and Product Development Department. Now that students have practiced with some complicated memos, challenge them to respond to this memo on their own. Be ready to support students. Remember, they are working at least one grade level ahead of their typical math curriculum and may have very little experience with applying math to graphic design and engineering tasks.

Memo

From: Design and Product Development Department

To: Engineering Team

Please calculate the cylinder's surface area for the jellyfish flyer so the Manufacturing Team can start calculating the costs.

Our sketch follows:

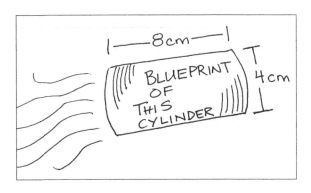

Calculating Surface Area of a Cylinder

$Area = 2\pi rh + 2\pi r^2$

π = pi = 3.14
r = radius
h = height

Work Area

Check your answer with an online calculation tool.

Memo

From: Design and Product Development Department

To: Engineering and Graphic Design Teams

In order for the surface area to be accurate, you must subtract out the "holes" in the flier's tube ends. There is no surface on a hole! Remember, the surface area of a circle is $A = \pi r^2$.

- ◆ What is the surface area of the tube with the "hole" ends (circles) subtracted out?

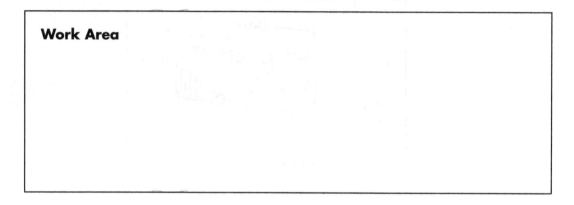

Work Area

- ◆ We will wrap cool decals around the sides of the Jellyfish Flier tubes to make them fun to own and collect.
- ◆ In order to create designs for the decals on the sides of the flier, we need accurate-sized "wraps." Calculate the exact size of the "decorative wraps" on your own paper.
- ◆ Draw and design three accurately sized "wraps" for the Jellyfish Fliers on a separate piece of paper, but add 3 cm to the length so the wraps can be taped together to wrap around the tube without any problems!

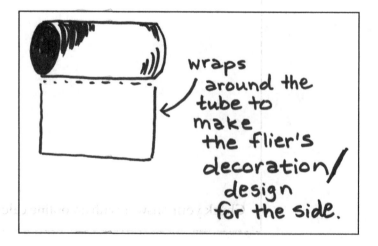

wraps around the tube to make the flier's decoration/ design for the side.

Teacher Notes

Calculating the Surface Area of the Cylinder Flier (Rounding pi to 3.14)

$(2 \times 3.14 \times 2 \times 8) + (2 \times 3.14 \times 2^2) =$
$100.48 + 25.12 = 125.60 \text{ cm}^2$

Subtracting Out the "Holes" or Circles on the Tube's Ends

$(3.14 \times 2^2) \times 2 \text{ holes} = 25.12 \text{ cm}^2$

Notice the number derived from subtracting out the holes (directly above) is the same as the second part of the equation for calculating the surface area $(2 \times 3.14 \times 2^2)$.

Our tube flier's surface area, minus the circular "holes," is the same as the first part of the equation: 100.48 cm^2.

Will the kids notice this?

How does this help explain the equation for calculating a cylinder's surface area?

Answer: The surface area of a cylinder includes the circular top and bottom of the cylinder. These circles are the two "holes" at the end of our tubes—the same holes we removed from our surface area calculation.

The Surface Area of the Wrap

Circumference × Length
Circumference = $2\pi r = 2 \times 3.14 \times 2 = 12.56 \text{ cm}$
$12.56 \text{ cm} \times 8 \text{ cm (length)} = 100.48 \text{ cm}^2$

Wait a minute! We're seeing a trend here! This is the first part of the cylinder equation! Will the kids notice, and can they explain?

And now we know the proper dimensions of a "wrap"—12.56 cm × 8 cm.

Lesson 1.4 Creating "Wraps" or Decals for the Jellyfish Fliers

In lesson 1.4, students will become graphic artists in order to create the most interesting designs for the Jellyfish Fliers.

Materials

- Handout: "Memo to Graphic Design Team"
- Construction paper
- T-squares and rulers
- Markers and/or colored pencils

Estimated Time

40–60 minutes

Procedure

Distribute the memo from the Graphic Design Team. Students will create three designs for the decals that will decorate the fliers.

In order to create accurately fitted "wraps," students should first use T-squares to draw 8-cm × 15-cm rectangles.

At least one of the designs should be a tessellation. For tips on how to make tessellations, watch this video:

How to Make a Tessalation – the Easy Way

www.youtube.com/watch?v=Ca5J_moee7U

Memo to Graphic Design Team

Design three different "wraps" or decals for the Jellyfish Flier. Be sure to make the wraps the proper size for prototypes and with an extra 3 cm in length for "wrapping" connections. Our exact calculations did not leave enough room for the wraps to overlap slightly; therefore, please design 8-cm × 15-cm wraps instead of exact calculations from the previous activity.

Bonus: Design at least one wrap as a tessellation. The tessellation will need to be a very small repeating pattern to fit on the wraps.

The preceding are a few samples (the last is slightly cut off).
The center and bottom samples are tessellations.
Make sure you draw the wraps accurately with 90-degree corners before you design them.

Lesson 1.5 Jellyfish Flier Prototypes

It's time to assemble a Jellyfish Flier and test it out. Be ready for cool-looking cardboard tubes flying around your classroom.

Materials

- Cardboard tube (from the center of a roll of paper towels, for example) cut down to 8 cm in length each, one per student
- Thin ribbon for the tendrils (3-mm or 1/8"-wide polyester ribbon, or ribbon of similar size; see photos)
- Small paper clips
- Tape
- Handout: "Memo from Design and Product Development Department"

Estimated Time

20–30 minutes

Procedure

Hand out the memo. Students use the memo's instructions, the decals they've created, the sample photos, and the prototype drawing to make a Jellyfish Flier.

Experiment with different numbers of paper clips and different lengths of ribbon to produce the best fliers.

Memo

From: Design and Product Development Department

To: Engineering Team

Make a Jellyfish Flier prototype of your best design. You will need these materials:

- ◆ Cardboard tube cut down to 8 cm in length
- ◆ Thin ribbon for the tendrils (as shown below)
- ◆ Small paper clips
- ◆ Tape
- ◆ The wraps you've designed

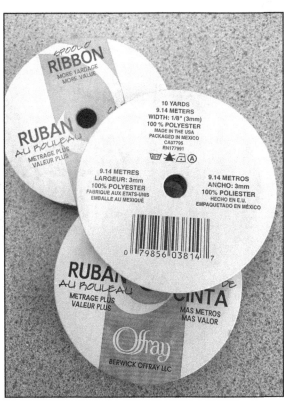

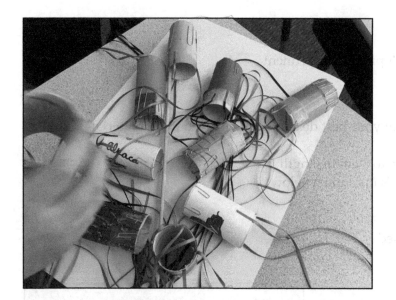

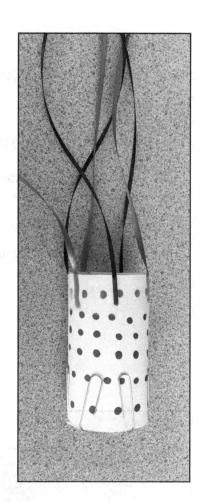

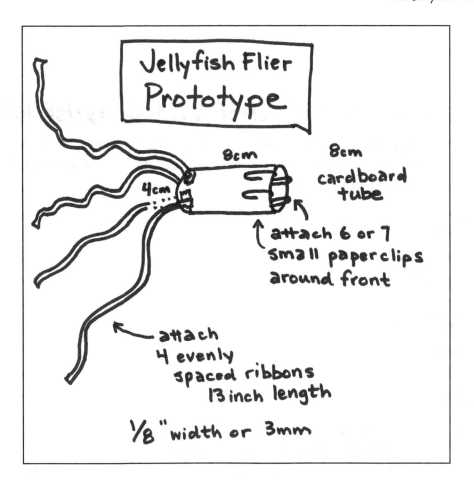

Throw the Tubes Like You Would Throw a Football

Some experiments have been done with the fliers that show adding more ribbons or more paper clips can be fine. Feel free to make adjustments so the tubes fly to your satisfaction.

Lesson 1.6 Data Collection With Jellyfish Fliers

In lesson 1.6, students throw their Jellyfish Fliers at a target and collect data that show how close the fliers landed to the target. The students then use the data and logical thinking to answer questions about carnival games.

Materials

- ◆ Paper and pencils
- ◆ Measuring tape

Estimated Time

30–40 minutes

Procedure

If students have been working at different paces throughout this unit, wait until all students have created a Jellyfish Flier prototype before continuing.

Distribute the memo from the Design and Product Development Department.

Memo

From: Design and Product Development Department

To: Engineering Team

We need to collect data for a game that might be played with the Jellyfish Fliers. Make a target at least 20 feet away, and then throw the fliers at the target. Record the distance the fliers land from the target to the nearest 1/4th foot.

It will work best if the whole group participates in this so that we gather a lot of data.

Repeat the process. Collect at least three sets of data.

With each set of data, calculate the range, mean, median, and mode distances from the target.

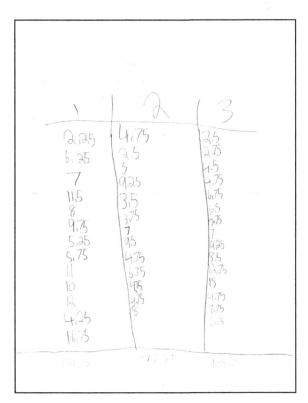
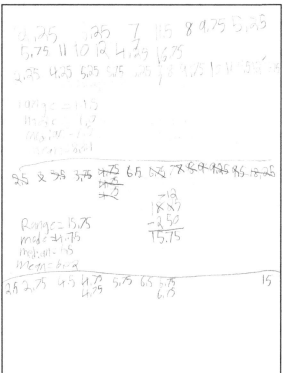

Now Answer These Questions

Why do we throw the fliers more than once when we collect data?

Let's say we were going to award prizes for really good throws—like in a carnival game. How could you use the range, the mean, the median, and the mode to decide when prizes should be awarded?

Teacher Notes

My students discovered (admittedly, because some did not follow directions) that variations of the prototypes work well—sometimes better—than the prototype pictured. Students had Jellyfish Fliers with six strings, short strings, six paper clips, big paper clips, and so on. Another student used a dowel for an atlatl to launch his flier. Yet another student used extra time to invent a rubber band launcher!

I had 15 students for the data collection portion. We went outside to throw the fliers. We stopped to record a set of data after one throw, and then we repeated the process two more times.

It was fortunate that the wind came up during the second throw of the fliers, as this got us thinking. Why should we collect more than one set of data? We had predicted that our throws would be better the second and third time, but they were worse because of the wind. This produced a good discussion about variables. We wouldn't have had this issue if we had thrown at a target in the hallway or in the gym.

Before we collected data, I explained we would measure to the nearest 1/4th foot. The students had to calculate 1/4th, 1/2, and 3/4th of a foot (3, 6, and 9 inches). I wanted to practice these common decimals: 0.75, 0.5, and 0.25 . . . so when I called out measurements, sometimes I would call out "3.75," other times "3 and three-quarters," and maybe "3 feet, 9 inches" the third time, and so on. I want the kids to be familiar with the variations of the terms and to be able to interpret and write all the variations in decimal form.

I showed the kids how to write their data set in order from smallest to largest—making it much easier to find the range, the median, and the mode. Once the data are written in this manner, it essentially becomes a bar graph. See the following example.

Now answer these questions:

Why do we throw the fliers more than once when we collect data?

The more data, the more accurate the mean becomes in predicting outcomes.

Let's say we were going to award prizes for really good throws—like in a carnival game. How could you use the range, the mean, the median, and the mode to decide when prizes will be awarded?

Answers vary. The range might help us determine special prizes. If a throw was 6 inches away—closer than any other throw in our range of data, then maybe a special prize will be awarded. The mode doesn't necessarily help us much with a carnival game; it gives us the most likely outcome. The median, like mode, doesn't help us much with a carnival game. The mean, however, definitely helps us determine prizes! We don't want to give away any prizes that are the result of throws worse than the mean. We will lose money!

Bonus Math Challenge—Using the Pythagorean Theorem

A Jellyfish Flier was thrown three times at the target (0,0). One toss landed in each quadrant, and a point was drawn where the flier landed.

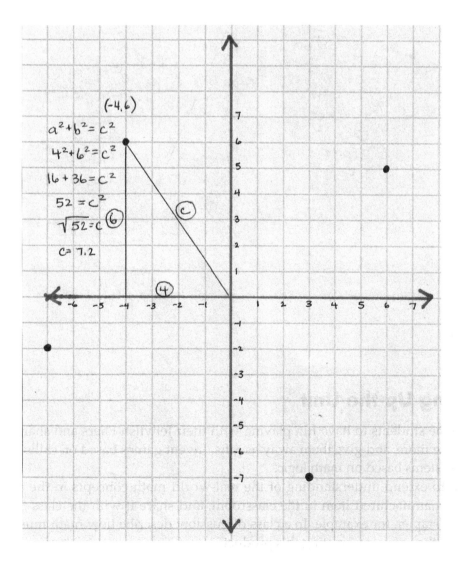

1. Label each point in each quadrant.
2. Use the x- and y-axis to create a right triangle with each point.
3. Use the Pythagorean theorem to calculate the displacement of the point from (0,0), and round to the nearest 10th.
4. A sample from Quadrant 4 has been completed.

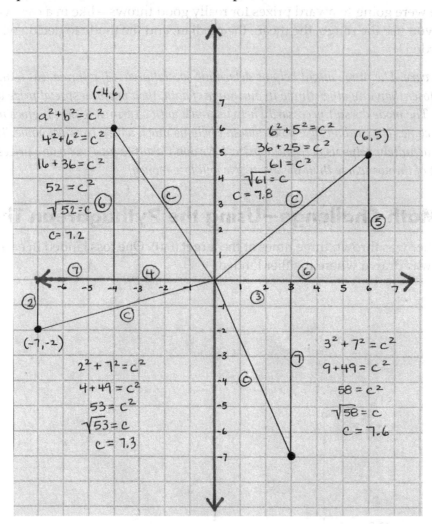

Answers

I = 7.2

II = 7.8

III = 7.6

IV = 7.3

Wrapping Up the Unit

Encourage the students to have fun playing with their Jellyfish Fliers and share them with friends. Make more, and give them away as gifts. Invent games based on skills in throwing and point systems based on math logic.

Finally, to extend understanding of the real-world math concepts in the unit, choose almost any manufactured item in the classroom, and share it with the class . . . a pair of scissors or a stapler, for example. In a class discussion, describe how math must have been important to the company creating this product.

Pikes Peak Math

Background

Loaded with hands-on, visual, real-world math challenges, this GATE math unit will challenge fourth- and fifth-grade students with new concepts across the curriculum. The unit is formatted so that it may be completed as an independent math challenge, as whole-class and small-group assignments, or even as a component of math *center* activities. Not just math—this unit crosses the curriculum for graphic design and drafting, historical primary sources, informative nonfiction, engineering, and economics.

Preparation Notes

As with Unit 1, The Jellyfish Flier, working through this unit as if you were a student is an excellent (and fun) way to prepare. The Jellyfish Flier will have served as outstanding training grounds for the drafting and technical drawing you and your young draftspersons and engineers will encounter in Pikes Peak Math.

Reserve a space where students working on this unit can store their projects. Collect the students' products into a portfolio. This portfolio will serve as an excellent addition to evidence for Advanced Learning Plans and as an excellent conversation piece for parent–teacher conferences. If students are working individually or at their own pace, their completed work may serve as examples to students who will encounter the challenges later on.

Unit Objective

The students will:

♦ Discover the relationship between mathematical scale and fractions.
♦ Calculate and use mean, median, and mode to produce clear representations of data.
♦ Use geometric principles and mathematical scale to create accurate physical models.
♦ Recognize mathematical patterns beyond their current grade level.

DOI: 10.4324/9781003257646-3

◆ Apply financial calculations and make real-world economic decisions.

◆ Apply math concepts creatively to produce an original product.

Active Common Core Math Standards Within This Unit

CCSS.MATH.CONTENT.6.G.A.1

Find the area of right triangles, other triangles, special quadrilaterals, and polygons by composing into rectangles or decomposing into triangles and other shapes; apply these techniques in the context of solving real-world and mathematical problems.

CCSS.MATH.CONTENT.6.G.A.3

Draw polygons in the coordinate plane given coordinates for the vertices; use coordinates to find the length of a side joining points with the same first coordinate or the same second coordinate. Apply these techniques in the context of solving real-world and mathematical problems.

CCSS.MATH.CONTENT.6.SP.B.4

Display numerical data in plots on a number line, including dot plots, histograms, and box plots.

CCSS.MATH.CONTENT.6.SP.B.5

Summarize numerical data sets in relation to their context, such as by:

CCSS.MATH.CONTENT.6.SP.B.5.A

Reporting the number of observations.

CCSS.MATH.CONTENT.6.SP.B.5.B

Describing the nature of the attribute under investigation, including how it was measured and its units of measurement.

CCSS.MATH.CONTENT.6.SP.B.5.C

Giving quantitative measures of center (median and/or mean) and variability (interquartile range and/or mean absolute deviation), as well as describing any overall pattern and any striking deviations from the overall pattern with reference to the context in which the data were gathered.

CCSS.MATH.CONTENT.6.SP.B.5.D

Relating the choice of measures of center and variability to the shape of the data distribution and the context in which the data were gathered.

CCSS.MATH.CONTENT.6.RP.A.3

Use ratio and rate reasoning to solve real-world and mathematical problems, e.g., by reasoning about tables of equivalent ratios, tape diagrams, double number line diagrams, or equations.

CCSS.MATH.CONTENT.7.G.A.1

Solve problems involving scale drawings of geometric figures, including computing actual lengths and areas from a scale drawing and reproducing a scale drawing at a different scale.

CCSS.MATH.CONTENT.7.G.B.4

Know the formulas for the area and circumference of a circle and use them to solve problems; give an informal derivation of the relationship between the circumference and area of a circle.

CCSS.MATH.CONTENT.7.G.B.6

Solve real-world and mathematical problems involving area, volume and surface area of two- and three-dimensional objects composed of triangles, quadrilaterals, polygons, cubes, and right prisms.

Launch

Watch *The Ridge* (www.youtube.com/watch?v=xQ_IQS3VKjA) as cyclist extraordinaire Danny Macaskill navigates his bicycle over mountain ridges, across boulders, and even over a barbed-wire fence.

As this unit may be completed individually, within small pullout groups, or as a whole class, so too can this launch activity. If students are working individually or in small groups, they can watch the video on personal devices or computers; as a whole class, project the video onto a large screen if you have that capability. If this launch is completed by the whole class, it will take approximately 45 minutes—a long duration for a launch—but I believe the engagement it provides and the math dialogue generated will be worth the time.

View the video one time through and simply enjoy it. Allow the students to comment on the wonders within. Ask, "How do you think Danny Macaskill made it to the point where he could ride a bike so amazingly well?" Hopefully, students will talk about resilience, practice, and a willingness to stretch oneself. It's always a good idea to talk about a growth mindset with gifted learners when we get a chance.

Before watching a second time, ask the students to think about how they see MATH playing a part of the events in the video: "For example, I see many measurement calculations Danny Macaskill must be making in his mind as he rides across boulders and jumps over gaps."

Other examples students might generate and you may point out include the following:

- The geometry and mechanics of a bicycle, wheels, cogs, chains, and the way they work together. We could calculate the distance a bike will travel based on one revolution of a pedal in varying gear sprockets, for example.
- Elevation of mountains and other natural features even including sunrise, sunset, and tiny wave ripples in the water all have a mathematical basis
- The distance oars are pulled through water partly determines the distance the boat is propelled in the opposite direction. We could calculate how many oar strokes it might take to cross a lake.
- Even the video itself is framed in a specific ratio to fit the YouTube platform—along with the countless mathematical calculations and applications needed to make any digital technology work.

If we stretch our thinking, we see math is everywhere . . . and that's one of the main takeaways of the launch.

Furthermore, ask, "Do you think Danny Macaskill is consciously performing measurements and mathematical estimations while he is riding, or when he moves, does he have a *feel* for what is happening?"

This produces our second key takeaway: Math is all around us, but humans are necessarily making calculations consciously. Much of math is intuitive for us—especially if we are gifted mathematically—and we can have a feel for mathematical relationships in a similar way that Danny Macaskill has a feel for his bike rides.

In a transition to the unit, say, "We are about to challenge your math skills with other mountains. In this unit, I think you will see how math is all around us. The challenges won't be as great as Danny Macaskill's bike rides over ridges, but they won't be easy either. Remember how hard he must have worked to get to where he is. This unit is designed to stretch your math abilities, too. Sometimes you'll have to trust your math intuition, and sometimes you may need a bit of help. That's OK. That just means you are learning and growing. Good luck!"

Lesson 2.1 America's Mountain—Pikes Peak, Elevation 14,150 Feet

In this lesson, students will draw Pikes Peak and then accurately scale their drawing to show elevation lines every 1,000 feet. They'll make calculations based on equivalent fractions as well.

Here in Colorado Springs, we are fortunate to be able to look out the big front windows of our school and draw Pikes Peak sitting right there in front of us. Your students may use one of the three pictures provided or may easily find a good view of the peak online.

Materials

- ◆ Drawing paper
- ◆ Ruler with both centimeters and inches
- ◆ Handout: "America's Mountain—Pikes Peak"
- ◆ Photo of Pikes Peak, either online or included in this lesson

Estimated Time

60 minutes

Procedure

Distribute the handout "America's Mountain—Pikes Peak." Encourage the students to read the instructions on their own to begin the task.

As a teacher, I understand that some students will need only the written directions because I know they will persist and complete the challenge with little guidance. Throughout this unit, however, keep in mind that it may be exceptionally challenging for fourth-grade students in particular. Some of our gifted students are unfamiliar with multiple-step, hands-on challenges. They may have become accustomed to zipping through pages of calculations and recognizing patterns but less adept at slowing down, considering possibilities, and applying skills. Some of the strongest "calculators" in my groups have been the first to want to abandon this project. Here's our chance to teach resilience once again.

> *For students needing tips or encouragement*: use centimeters and not inches when creating your scaled measurements. It's much easier to scale using the metric system. Work from the top of the mountain down. Don't label the bottom of the drawing as 6,000 feet yet. Align your ruler and see where elevation lines might be drawn, making sure 6,000 feet will appear somewhere near the bottom of your page.

How Do I Grade This Unit?

The short answer is that you don't. I have taught fourth- and fifth-grade gifted students for more than 20 years. When immersed in working on engaging projects, not once has a student asked about a grade. As a teacher, you will know when a student has successfully completed a task for this unit and is ready to move on to the next challenge: guide, encourage, revise if necessary, and then move on. In each step, let the students interact with the challenge—struggle if necessary a bit—before you step in as a kindly tour guide. I've always felt that my job as a teacher of gifted students is to inspire a challenge and then get out of the way. If you must grade this project as a part of reporting requirements, I suggest that all completed projects be given an A+ or Exceeds Standards for working one or two or more grade levels ahead.

Checking for Successful Completion

Make sure the students have drawn clear elevation lines and that the lines are spaced at an accurate scale. A ruler with centimeters and logical-mathematical thinking will be required. A sample is included.

1/8th of the elevation between 6,000 and 14,000 feet = 1,000 feet.
1/16th of the elevation between 6,000 and 14,000 feet = 500 feet.
6/32nd (or 3/16th) of the elevation is 1,500 feet.

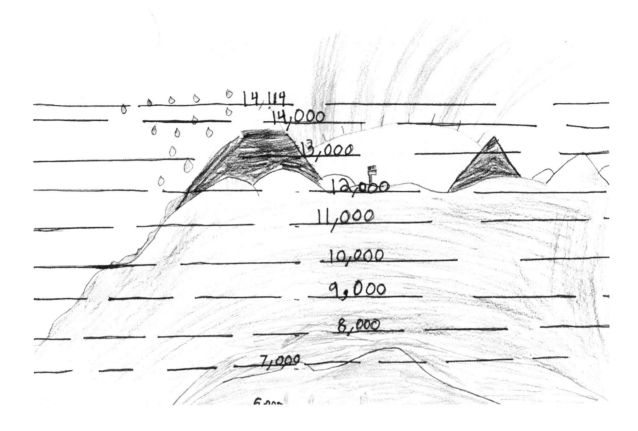

From the Common Core

CCSS.Math.Content.4.NF.B.3
Understand a fraction a/b with $a > 1$ as a sum of fractions $1/b$.

CCSS.Math.Content.4.NF.B.3.a
Understand addition and subtraction of fractions as joining and separating parts referring to the same whole.

CCSS.Math.Content.4.NF.B.3.b
Decompose a fraction into a sum of fractions with the same denominator in more than one way, recording each decomposition by an equation. Justify decompositions, e.g., by using a visual fraction model. *Examples: 3/8 = 1/8 + 1/8 + 1/8; 3/8 = 1/8 + 2/8; 2 1/8 = 1 + 1 + 1/8 = 8/8 + 8/8 + 1/8.*

CCSS.Math.Content.4.NF.B.3.d
Solve word problems involving addition and subtraction of fractions referring to the same whole and having like denominators, e.g., by using visual fraction models and equations to represent the problem.

CCSS.Math.Content.5.NF.A.2
Solve word problems involving addition and subtraction of fractions referring to the same whole, including cases of unlike denominators, e.g., by using visual fraction models or equations to represent the problem. Use benchmark fractions and number sense of fractions to estimate mentally and assess the reasonableness of answers.

Following the student directions are Pikes Peak reference photos.

America's Mountain—Pikes Peak

At 14,114 feet in elevation, Pikes Peak is the most visited mountain in North America and the second-most visited mountain in the world.

In this activity, you will show your understanding of fractions and the addition and subtraction of fractions and will work with fractions to solve a real-world problem using a visual model.

Here is what you'll do:

Elevation Graphic Design Challenge

◆ Using a standard sheet of drawing paper (although larger is OK), draw a view of Pikes Peak using the picture your teacher provides. It doesn't matter if you orient your drawing paper vertically or horizontally. It is important, however, that you draw the actual peak of Pikes Peak near the top of the page with at least one inch to spare.

◆ Make sure the top of Pikes Peak is labeled as 14,114 feet.

◆ Clearly draw elevation lines from 6,000 feet to 14,000 feet. Measure the lines and space them accurately using centimeters. Each 1,000 feet line must be the same distance from the line above and below—beginning at the bottom of the page and continuing to 14,000 feet. For a more difficult challenge, use inches instead of centimeters.

◆ Label all elevation lines clearly. Add a title.

◆ Answer these questions:

• How many feet is 1/8 of the elevation between 6,000 feet and 14,000 feet?
• How many feet is 1/16 of the elevation between 6,000 feet and 14,000 feet?
• How many feet is 6/32 of the elevation between 6,000 feet and 14,000 feet?

Source: From WikiMedia Commons: https://commons.wikimedia.org/wiki/File:Pikes_Peak_from_Garden_of_the_Gods.JPG

Source: From WikiMedia Commons: https://commons.wikimedia.org/wiki/File:Pikes_Peak_by_David_Shankbone.jpg

Lesson 2.2 Elevation and Temperature

In this activity, students will read an excerpt that contains temperature readings at different elevations. They'll construct a table from the readings and calculate the mean temperature change between elevations. Finally, students will construct a small poster to show their results.

We transform language into numbers, numbers into a table, and calculations into graphic design. It's a pretty cool waltz across the curriculum!

Materials

- Drawing paper, one sheet per student
- Markers and/or colored pencils
- Ruler or straight edge
- Handout: "Elevation and Temperature"

Estimated Time

60–90 minutes

Procedure

Distribute the handout "Elevation and Temperature." All of my fifth graders needed a refresher on mean, median, and mode the last time I taught this lesson. Fourth graders may not have encountered these terms. Be prepared to explain.

Checking for Successful Completion

The temperature changes at each elevation are as follows:

6,000 to 7,000 feet = 5.4 degrees
7,000 to 8,000 feet = 5.1 degrees
8,000 to 9,000 feet = 5.7 degrees
9,000 to 10,000 feet = 6.0 degrees
10,000 to 11,000 feet = 4.8 degrees
11,000 to 12,000 feet = 5.4 degrees
12,000 to 13,000 feet = 5.6 degrees
13,000 to 14,000 feet = 5.2 degrees

The median temperature change is 5.4.

The mode is 5.4.
The mean is 5.4.

Did You Know?

Every tim you go up or down 1,000 feet in elevation the temperature goes up or down 5.4 °F degrees.

Check out
JwubrickenziesawesomE.com
{McKenzie's has the facts}

America's Mountain Pikes Peak is 14,114 feet in elevation. Research done by proves this is correct.

Pikes Peak

Elevation	Temperature	Temperature Changes
6,000 ft	88 °F	5.4 °F
7,000 ft	82.6 °F	5.1 °F
8,000 ft	77.5 °F	5.7 °F
9,000 ft	71.8 °F	6.0 °F
10,000 ft	65.8 °F	4.8 °F
11,000 ft	61.0 °F	5.4 °F
12,000 ft	55.6 °F	5.6 °F
13,000 ft	50.0 °F	5.2 °F
14,000 ft	44.8 °F	
Mode	mean	median
5.4 °F	5.4	5.4

From the Common Core

CCSS.Math.Content.4.MD.A.2
Use the four operations to solve word problems involving distances, intervals of time, liquid volumes, masses of objects, and money, including problems involving simple fractions or decimals, and problems that require expressing measurements given in a larger unit in terms of a smaller unit. Represent measurement quantities using diagrams such as number line diagrams that feature a measurement scale.

CCSS.Math.Content.5.NBT.B.7
Add, subtract, multiply, and divide decimals to hundredths, using concrete models or drawings and strategies based on place value, properties of operations, and/or the relationship between addition and subtraction; relate the strategy to a written method and explain the reasoning used.

CCSS.Math.Content.6.SP.B.5.c
Giving quantitative measures of center (median and/or mean) and variability (interquartile range and/or mean absolute deviation), as well as describing any overall pattern and any striking deviations from the overall pattern with reference to the context in which the data were gathered.

Elevation and Temperature

In this activity, you take a closer look at elevations and use your skills with adding and subtracting decimals along with calculations to find a mean in a set of data. First, read the following excerpt.

A Chilly Journey up the Mountain on a Summer's Day

As we rode the Cog Railway from Manitou Springs toward Pikes Peak, I used my smartphone to take temperature readings at different elevations.

- At 6,000 feet, the temperature was 88 degrees Fahrenheit.
- At 7,000 feet, the temperature was 82.6 degrees Fahrenheit.
- At 8,000 feet, the temperature was 77.5 degrees Fahrenheit.
- At 9,000 feet, the temperature was 71.8 degrees Fahrenheit.
- At 10,000 feet, the temperature was 65.8 degrees Fahrenheit.
- At 11,000 feet, the temperature was 61.0 degrees Fahrenheit.
- At 12,000 feet, the temperature was 55.6 degrees Fahrenheit.
- At 13,000 feet, the temperature was 50.0 degrees Fahrenheit.
- Near the Summit of Pikes Peak at 14,000 feet, the temperature was 44.8 degrees Fahrenheit.

Wow! It's a good thing I brought my jacket!

- Use the temperatures and elevations to make a three-column table that clearly shows elevations, temperature readings, and changes in temperature.
- Calculate the median and the mode decrease in temperature. Show your work.
- Calculate the mean decrease in temperature. Show your work.
- Use the mean decrease in temperature to make a small poster that educates others about the mathematical relationship between elevation and temperature change. Use a clear title and include a graphic/drawing to make your poster more attractive. Imagine the poster might be placed at the bottom of a railway that goes to the top of Pikes Peak. We want tourists to know what temperature changes they can expect.

Lesson 2.3 Peak Primary Sources

Here is a critical thinking cross-curricular piece for real-world applications and analysis of primary sources. It will provide a strong background for the engineering task of making a model railroad cog in the next lesson as students analyze primary source photos.

Materials

◆ Handout: "Primary Sources"
◆ Handout: "The Manitou and Pikes Peak Cog Railway"

Estimated Time

40 minutes

Procedure

This lesson comes with a warning label.

Distribute the handout "Primary Sources." Although this lesson does not include specific Common Core State Standards in math, interpreting primary sources serves as a best practice in social studies/history. Standards in Common Core Language Arts and "close reading" skills also apply as they're used here—particularly in looking for details and in making inferences and interpretations. Interpretations of primary sources take an eye for details and strong critical thinking skills—all of which provide challenge and skill building for gifted learners.

In addition, a couple of the questions require the students to consider economic implications (economics is in the social studies standards in my state)—undoubtedly a strong connection with mathematical-logical thought.

All of this being said, let's be careful not to derail mathematically gifted students with this lesson. Over the years, many of my mathematically gifted students exhibit large gaps between their quantitative and verbal abilities. As teachers who provide challenges for gifted learners, we understand that it's our job to enhance a student's strengths. While developing weaker academic areas is an essential part of a student's growth, it may not be a vital part of your mission within your gifted groups. If a student with large gaps between verbal–quantitative skills only sees you 1 or 2 hours a week in an enrichment group, it will be smart to make adjustments in this lesson. You may do so by completing the tasks in this lesson together as a whole group through discussion or by summarizing the key takeaways as a mini-lesson in historical background.

You may want to project or enlarge the photos (one is in color but it does not have to be printed that way). It worked fine for me when I simply printed and copied the images along with the questions. I displayed the postcard photo on my computer screen for students to look at if they wanted to see it in color. After the handouts are sample answers to the interpretive questions.

I definitely recommend visiting the Manitou and Pikes Peak Cog Railway website together with students once these activities have been completed.

Present this challenge in two separate pieces—beginning with the handout titled "Primary Sources." Do not distribute the handout titled "The Manitou and Pikes Peak Cog Railway" until the questions on the "Primary Sources" handout have been completed.

From the Common Core

CCSS.ELA-Literacy.RI.5.1
Quote accurately from a text when explaining what the text says explicitly and when drawing inferences from the text.

CCSS.ELA-Literacy.RI.5.7
Draw on information from multiple print or digital sources, demonstrating the ability to locate an answer to a question quickly or to solve a problem efficiently.

Primary Sources

Look very carefully at the details in the photo. What do you see? List details, but do not make interpretations or reach any conclusions about what is pictured here.

Where and when is this photo taken? How do you know? Use details.

How is this train different from others you've seen?

Cross-Reference: The photo shown is from a postcard published at about the same time as the previous photo. What similarities do you see?

Do you think the women in the photo were passengers on the train in the picture? Explain.

This photo is from a postcard—a very popular form of communication at one time. Why would the publishers of the postcard say that selling their postcards are great for local businesses?

The Manitou and Pikes Peak Cog Railway

You've seen gears before. You can find gears in clocks, in toys, and in all sorts of machines. Could gears like these be used as wheels to help a train make its way up a steep incline?

The Manitou and Pikes Peak Cog Railway was founded in 1889. Tourists had already been making the journey up Pikes Peak on pack mules, and the United States army had built a telegraph signal station at the 14,115-foot summit. Could there be a more comfortable and leisurely way for tourists to reach the summit of America's Mountain? A special railway might be the answer.

There was a problem. A typical railway would not be able to make the steep climbs from Manitou Springs to the summit, but a different sort of railway—one using cogs instead of just friction and smooth wheels—had been invented in New Hampshire in 1869. Cog railways include standard rails as well as an additional cog rack and rail in the middle beneath the train. This middle rack includes notches for gears—or cogs—which are fitted beneath the train. As the train makes its way up steep inclines, the middle cog and rack system hold the train in place, turning cogged wheels into the gears as it churns its way up a slope.

On June 30, 1891, the first cog railway train carried a Denver church choir to the Summit of Pikes Peak. Since then, thousands upon thousands of tourists have enjoyed the views from the Manitou and Pikes Peak Cog Railway and have enjoyed the famous donuts and hot chocolate available at the Summit House gift shop.

Inferences

Why do you think it took two years to build the Manitou and Pikes Peak Cog Railway? Do cog railways travel fast? Why or why not?

Why would someone want to build a railroad to the top of Pikes Peak? Make inferences, and cite evidence from the excerpt to support your answer.

Based on the written description, draw a picture of a cogwheel and track on the back of this paper.

Read more about the Manitou and Pikes Peak Cog Railway and view pictures: http://cograilway.com/about-the-train.asp

See an additional postcard of the cog train on the summit of Pikes Peak here: https://tile.loc.gov/storage-services/service/pnp/ppmsca/18200/18299v.jpg

Primary Sources—Sample Answers

Source: www.loc.gov/pictures/item/2016808853/

Look very carefully at the details in the photo. What do you see? List details, but do not make interpretations or reach any conclusions about what is pictured here.

Manitou and Pikes Peak Railway on the passenger car. Looks like sky in the background. Rocky. No plants. Engine behind passenger car. Black and white. Smokestack. Notches in the rails. Big windows in the passenger car.

Where and when is this photo taken? How do you know? Use details.

It is probably near Pikes Peak. It is possibly above timberline with no plants and just bare sky in the background of the picture. I see the words printed on the passenger car. This must be a long time ago. Newer trains don't have smokestacks, and if this were modern, it would probably be in color.

How is this train different from others you've seen?

The notches in the track, three rails, and the engine pushing the passenger car are all differences. Modern trains do not have a smokestack.

Source: www.loc.gov/pictures/item/2016808853/

Cross-Reference: The photo shown is from a postcard published at about the same time as the previous photo. What similarities do you see?

I see the notched track much more clearly in this photo. It looks like it might be the same train in the distance, and it definitely looks like it is high on a mountain. Also, there are no trees to be seen, probably very high on a mountain. The women's clothing is old-fashioned—Victorian clothing. It's a long time ago.

Do you think the women in the photo were passengers on the train in the picture? Explain.

The women may have been passengers on the train. It looks like there is a wooden platform and step stool which they used to step off the passenger car.

This photo is from a tourist's postcard—a very popular form of communication at one time. Why would the publishers of the postcard say, "This is great for business!"

The postcard would be sent off, and those receiving it would think that this place is really spectacular. They would want to visit this place, too. When they visit, they will spend money. That's great advertising!

The Manitou and Pikes Peak Cog Railway—Sample Answers

You've seen gears before. You can find gears in clocks, in toys, and in all sorts of machines. Could gears like these be used as wheels to help a train make its way up a steep incline?

The Manitou and Pikes Peak Cog Railway was founded in 1889. Tourists had already been making the journey up Pikes Peak on pack mules, and the U.S. Army had built a telegraph signal station at the 14,115-foot summit. Could there be a more comfortable and leisurely way for tourists to reach the summit of America's Mountain? A special railway might just be the answer.

There was a problem. A typical railway would not be able to make the steep climbs from Manitou Springs to the summit, but a different sort of railway—one using cogs instead of just friction and smooth wheels—had been invented in New Hampshire in 1869. Cog railways include standard rails as well as an additional cog rack and rail in the middle beneath the train. This middle rack includes notches for gears—or cogs—which are fitted beneath the train. As the train makes its way up steep inclines, the middle cog and rack system hold the train in place, turning cogged wheels into the gears as it churns its way up a slope.

On June 30, 1891, the first cog railway train carried a church choir from Denver to the Summit of Pikes Peak. Since then, thousands upon thousands of tourists have enjoyed the views from the Manitou and Pikes Peak Cog Railway and have enjoyed the famous donuts and hot chocolate available at the Summit House gift shop.

Inferences

Why do you think it took two years to build the Manitou and Pikes Peak Cog Railway?

It was built on a rugged mountain at a high elevation. It must have been difficult to get building supplies onto the slopes and to clear a path through steep, rocky, and wooded areas.

Do cog railways travel fast? Why or why not?

Probably not. The cogs have to lock in place safely. If the train moves too fast, the cogs could slip unsafely.

Would someone want to build such a railway just to see if it could be done? What are other reasons could there be? Cite evidence from the excerpt to support your answer.

Money could be made from selling tickets to tourists who want to go to the top of Pikes Peak. The article mentions tourists, and tourists spend money. It would cost a lot to build the railway. It wouldn't be done just for fun. If there is a gift shop at the summit, then it is a place made for tourists.

Lesson 2.4 Cog Spinner Geometry and Design Challenge

In this part of the lesson, students will have to work with precision, use measuring tools, geometric knowledge, and follow written instructions in order to construct a cog-shaped spinner. We will use these cog spinners in the next lesson—A Day Skiing in the Colorado Mountains.

Materials

- ◆ 2 white sheets of construction paper
- ◆ 1 sheet of construction paper, any light color other than white
- ◆ Compass or very large circle template (even a large circular lid like a coffee can lid)
- ◆ Ruler
- ◆ Pencil
- ◆ Protractor
- ◆ Tape and scissors
- ◆ Multipage handout—"Cog Spinner Geometry and Design Challenge"

Estimated Time

45 minutes

Procedure

Make sure to try this lesson out for yourself first. You'll be more familiar with the process and the possible frustrations the students have. My fourth and fifth graders did a very good job with this design; however, they did have questions along the way.

Tip: If students get confused, tell the kids to read ahead in the directions so they can get a big picture.
Tip: Substitute a large coffee can lid instead of drawing with a compass.

With this lesson, we cross over into other skill areas dependent on logical-mathematical thinking with our drafting and graphic design tasks. Engineers, graphic designers, architects, and designers in all areas use these same skills.

From the Common Core

CCSS.Math.Content.4.MD.C.6
Measure angles in whole-number degrees using a protractor. Sketch angles of specified measure.

CCSS.Math.Content.6.G.A.3
Draw polygons in the coordinate plane given coordinates for the vertices; use coordinates to find the length of a side joining points with the same first coordinate or the same second coordinate. Apply these techniques in the context of solving real-world and mathematical problems.

CCSS.Math.Content.7.G.A.2
Draw (freehand, with ruler and protractor, and with technology) geometric shapes with given conditions. Focus on constructing triangles from three measures of angles or sides, noticing when the conditions determine a unique triangle, more than one triangle, or no triangle.

Cog Spinner Geometry and Design Challenge

In this activity, you'll construct a spinner using measuring tools. In order to make an accurate and attractive cog spinner, you'll need to draw carefully. Be precise. Keep an eraser handy. You may have to start over one or more times. Read and follow the instructions carefully. It's a good idea to look through the entire set of instructions before you begin so that you know what your finished product will look like.

Materials

- 2 white sheets of construction paper
- 1 sheet of construction paper, any light color other than white
- Compass or very large circle template (even a large circular lid like a coffee can lid)
- Ruler
- Pencil
- Protractor

Instructions

Orient one white sheet of construction paper horizontally. With your compass or circle template, draw a circle that spans most of the paper, top to bottom. Make sure to leave about 4 centimeters of empty space at the top and the bottom.

Using a ruler, make note of the diameter of the circle. This one is 16 centimeters. Now add an additional centimeter to the diameter on both the top and the bottom. That makes 18 centimeters for this circle. Make a note of your measurement: diameter plus 2 centimeters.

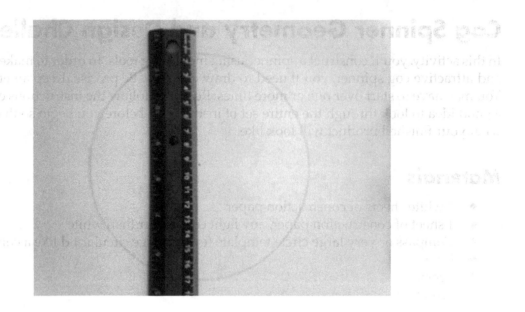

Now use your second sheet of white construction paper to make a template you'll use to draw cogs onto your circle. Orient the paper horizontally, and measure carefully from the top edge. Mark a point 3 centimeters down from the top edge of the paper.

Make another 3-centimeter mark from the top edge of the page. You should now have two 3-centimeter marks from the top edge of the paper.

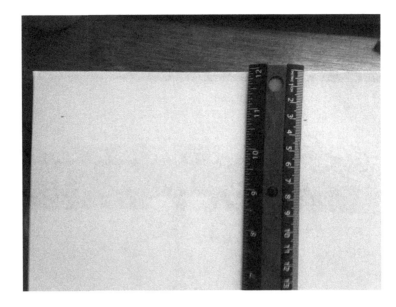

Carefully connect the two marks with a line segment (draw the line segment so that it covers most of the length of the page). Make sure to use your ruler. You will now have a line segment across most of the top of your page at 3 centimeters from the top.

Measure along the line segment to a length equal to the diameter of your circle plus two centimeters, and mark this point. Remember, my circle's diameter plus 2 equaled 18

centimeters. I've placed a point along the line segment I've just drawn at the 18-centimeter mark.

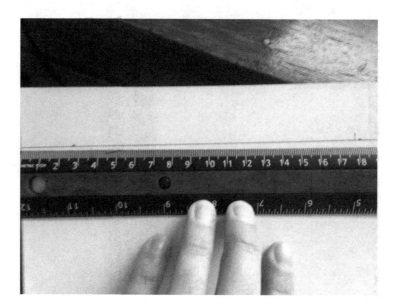

Draw another point along the top edge of the paper at the same distance (18 centimeters from the edge for me), and connect the two points using your ruler. You should now have drawn a perfect rectangle that is 3 centimeters wide and your circle's diameter plus 2 centimeters in length.

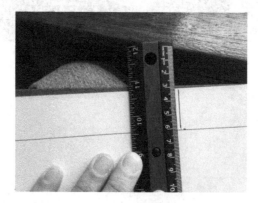

Cut out your rectangle carefully. Keep the edges as straight as possible! Once again, this rectangle should be the diameter of your circle plus 2 centimeters long by 3 centimeters wide.

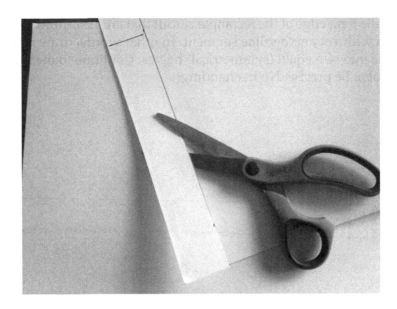

Now use your ruler to draw lines segments across the rectangle one centimeter from each edge. Both of these line segments should be exactly one centimeter from the long edges of the rectangle. The middle rectangle's long side should equal to the diameter of your circle.

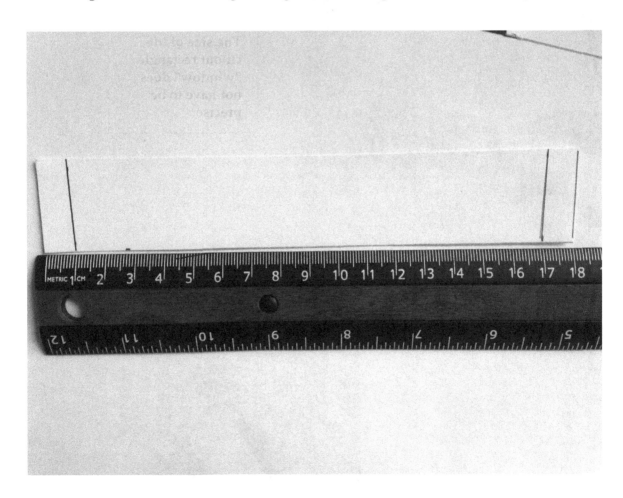

Mark points near the long edge of the rectangle cutout that are 1.5 centimeters from the edge, and connect them with yet another line segment. In other words, draw a line segment that splits the rectangle into two equal (symmetrical) halves. Continue to measure precisely and draw with your ruler. Be precise. No freehanding!

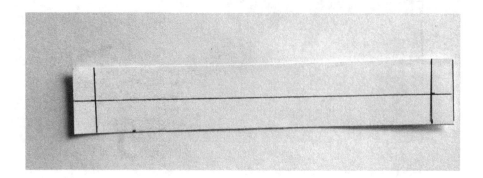

Fold the rectangle in half, and cut a small rectangle from the folds. Unfold it again. You have now constructed a very handy template that you'll use to draw the cogs onto the circle.

> **The size of the cutout rectangle "window" does not have to be precise.**

No go back to the first sheet of white construction paper where you've drawn a circle. We're about to use the template we just made—the one rectangle with the little window cut out of its middle—to draw a cog.

Using a ruler, draw a diagonal across the circle. Make sure this diagonal crosses through the center point of the circle.

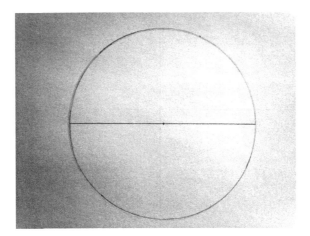

Using a protractor, mark a point at exactly a 90-degree angle above and below the diagonal.

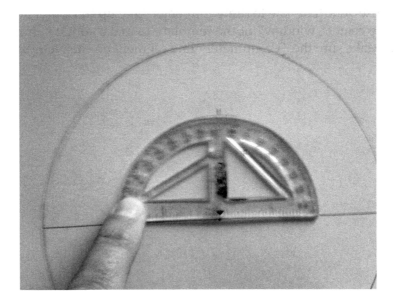

Carefully draw a line segment through the points to separate your circle into four equal quadrants.

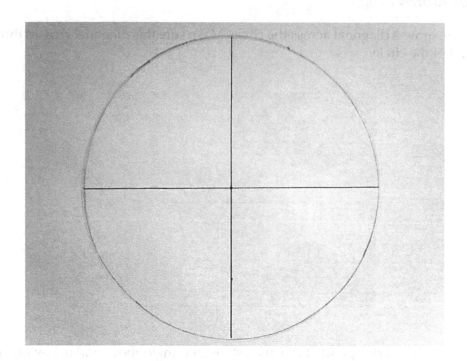

You are ready to use your template to draw four cogs. Line up the template along one of the diagonals. Use the center "window" of the template to make sure it's lined up all the way across the circle. Make sure the "1 centimeter" line segment on each template is a tangent to the circle.

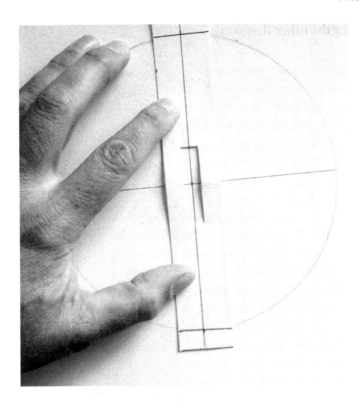

Use the template to draw a cog on each end. Take your time. You may want to tape the template on top of the circle if it helps.

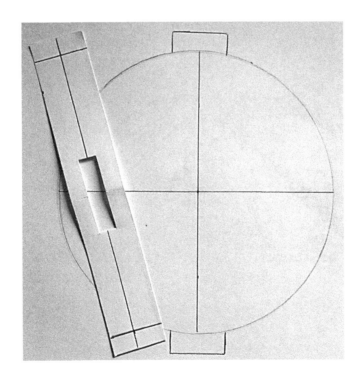

Repeat the process for the other diagonal.

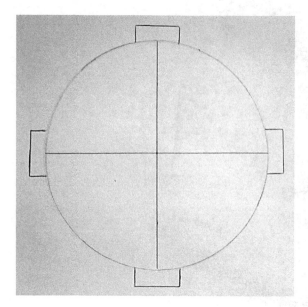

Now carefully measure and mark 45-degree points in each of the four quadrants you've already drawn.

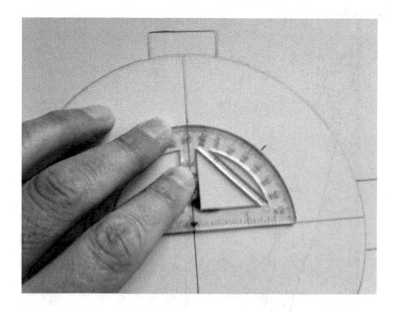

Draw two more diagonals through these four points. Oops! Did you measure correctly? You'll know if you've made a mistake if your line segment does not pass through the center point of the circle or if your "slice of pie" in the circle does not look the same size. Don't worry if you've made a mistake. This is why pencils come with erasers.

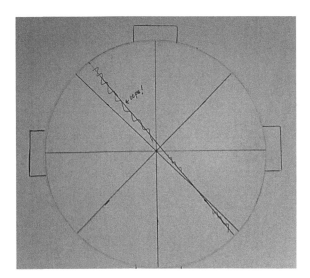

Use your template to draw the remaining four cogs, carefully cut around the edges, and you're ready to complete the cog spinner.

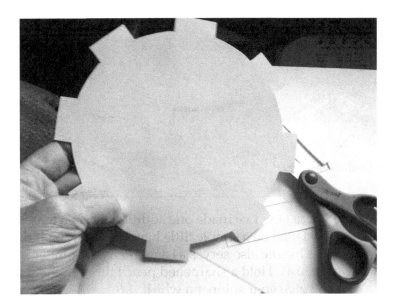

Poke a hole through the center point of the cog, but be careful with sharp objects!

Lay the cog onto a light-colored sheet of construction paper. Keep it steady. You may want to tape it onto the light-colored construction paper temporarily for this process. Between the cogs, neatly write different dollar values as shown.

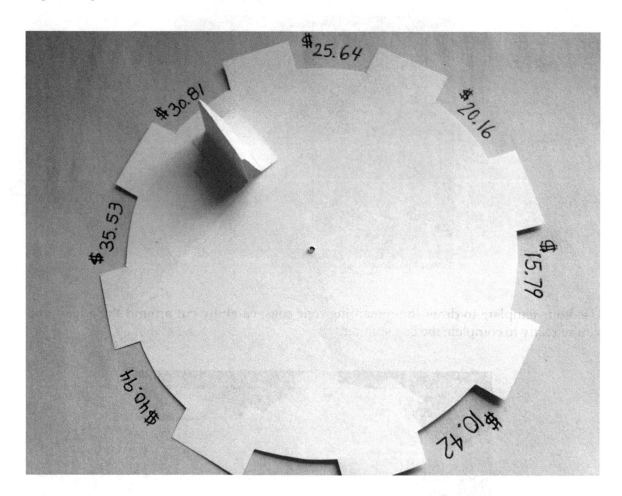

Label With These Dollar Values

- $5.25
- $10.42
- $15.79
- $20.16
- $25.64
- $30.81
- $35.53
- $40.94

Notice how I've made one addition. From a leftover scrap, I've taped on a simple little handle to make spinning easier. This handle also serves as a marker. My spinner is pointing to $30.81. Hold a sharpened pencil through the center point, and give your spinner a whirl!

Lesson 2.5 Spin for Money

In lesson 2.5, students practice with mean, median, and mode again as they put their spinners to practical use to accumulate money for a Colorado ski trip.

Materials

◆ Handout: "Spin for Money"
◆ Handout: "Breckenridge Ski Trip Tally Sheet"

Estimated Time

20–30 minutes

Procedure

Using the spinner they've created from the cogwheel, students will spin 10 times and record the dollar amounts on their handout "Spin for Money."

The handout will instruct the students to keep a running total of their dollar values and then calculate the mean, the median, and the mode of the data gathered through the 10 spins.

The median is a bit tricky for this one since there is an even number of dollar amounts. If the two middle numbers (the fifth and sixth in this series of 10 numbers) are different, the median is found by finding the average/mean of the fifth and sixth numbers. For example, if the two middle numbers were 4 and 6, the median would be 5.

Alert students will realize that all they have to do to find the mean is move the decimal one place to the left since we are dividing by 10. If students do not see this, point it out to them—as it is a fifth-grade Common Core State Standard.

Answers will vary for the mean, median, and mode. Just a note: it will be impossible for students to have a total of less than $52.50 or more than $409.40. Most of my students had between $200 and $250 after the spins. This is important for the multistep word problems because students are not intended to have enough money to pay for the ski trip and must place a balance on a credit card.

From the Common Core

CCSS.Math.Content.5.NBT.A.2
Explain patterns in the number of zeros of the product when multiplying a number by powers of 10, and explain patterns in the placement of the decimal point when a decimal is multiplied or divided by a power of 10. Use whole-number exponents to denote powers of 10.

"Spin for Money"

- ◆ Spin the cog spinner 10 times, and record the dollar amounts.
- ◆ Write the sum of the dollar amounts, and keep a running total in the right column.
- ◆ Farther down, write the dollar amounts of each spin in order, and then calculate the mean, the median, and the mode.

Spin Number	Total of Spin	Running Total Dollar Amount of Spins
1		
2		
3		
4		
5		
6		
7		
8		
9		
10		

Mode	Median	Mean

Work Area: Write the 10 dollar amounts of spins, in order to make it easier to locate the mode and the median:

Lesson 2.6 A Day Skiing in the Colorado Mountains

On their ski trip, students will use the money they've accumulated from spinning the cog spinners. Along the way, they'll need to make real-world calculations and financial decisions. These classic multistep word problems require addition, subtraction, multiplication, and division to the hundredths place value, percentage discounts, and logical-mathematical thinking. In an economics extension, students calculate compound interest for 12 months on a credit card.

Materials

Handout: "A Day Skiing in the Colorado Mountains"

Estimated Time

40 minutes, with some students completing the word problems much more quickly

Procedure

Distribute the handout "A Day Skiing in the Colorado Mountains."

Students need to keep a note of the total they've made from the 10 spins with their cog spinners. This is the money they have available for a Colorado ski vacation. Challenging multistep problems lead the students through the finances of a day on the slopes. Allow the students to struggle with math problems beyond their grade level. Allow their natural mathematical intuition and strong abilities of math logic to guide them . . . but absolutely be ready to teach and guide students through what should be new mathematical concepts! Once again, we have an opportunity for gifted mathematicians to wrangle with the uncomfortable feeling of not being able to "get it" with a snap of the fingers. This isn't a "gotcha" but an opportunity to grow in a safe space of the gifted and talented classroom. A tally sheet helps students keep track of expenses. Solutions to the multistep problems appear later.

Students are about to dive into seventh-grade math standards with several percentage calculations. Because I don't want these calculations to become tedious bookwork or math worksheets (this is no "gotcha" exercise or math punishment), I encourage my fourth and fifth graders to use a calculator. With a little instruction from me, mathematically gifted students develop a good grasp of percentages. They already understand fractions and decimals, so percentage calculations are not a huge leap. Although it may be fun for some students to walk through paper and pencil calculations of long division, the important new mathematical concepts in this lesson are an understanding of how math applies to real-world experiences and an understanding of percentages.

   At the end of the ski trip, students will be short of cash—as calculated on the handout "Breckenridge Ski Trip Tally Sheet." This is entirely by design. Like many of us, students will be left with a credit card payment at the end of the ski trip.

From the Common Core

CCSS.Math.Content.7.RP.A.3
Use proportional relationships to solve multistep ratio and percent problems. Examples: simple interest, tax, markups and markdowns, gratuities and commissions, fees, percent increase and decrease, percent error.

A Day Skiing in the Colorado Mountains

Multistep Word Problems

Using the money you've earned from spinning your "cog spinner," you are about to go on a ski adventure for yourself and a friend. Solve the multistep problems below to see how much this little outing will cost you. You have a credit card just in case you can't pay for all of it with your "spinner cash." In all problems, round to the nearest 100th. Record your answers, with totals and balances, on the Breckenridge Ski Trip Tally Sheet.

Your drive from Colorado Springs, Colorado, to Breckenridge, Colorado, will be 220 miles round trip.

You can drive 18.7 miles on one gallon of gas. You better make sure you've got enough gas before you go. Colorado Springs gas prices are $2.37 per gallon. How much money will you spend on gas?

You will need two lift tickets at the ski area. The lift tickets are $135.00 each. Luckily, you found a 20%-off coupon. What is the cost of the two lift tickets with the discount?

You found a good price on ski rentals. You will need an intermediate rental package and an expert rental package. One intermediate package will cost $17.56, and one expert package will cost $18.14. You decide to get rental insurance just in case. You never know what might happen, and you don't want to take the chance that you will have to pay for lost, damaged, or stolen skis. Insurance costs an additional 10% more than the total of the two packages. What is the total you've spent on rentals and insurance?

You're saving money by packing your lunch. The lunch total is $6.17. Whew . . . You sure had to get up early, though. You need a venti-sized coffee, and you're very particular about your coffee. It's going to cost you $7.77 (you wanted a scone, too). You have a 50%-off coupon for your dinner on the way home. The bill for dinner, before the discount, was $33.66. What is your food and beverage grand total for the day?

Maybe you shouldn't have browsed in the shops on the streets of Breckenridge, because you found a ski parka you just can't live without! You want to ski in style! Should you spend $149.00 on it? Why not! You just got "paid" with the spinner. What about the stocking cap, too? It's on sale for 15% of the price of the jacket. Well, it's simply too good of a deal to pass on. What is the total price of the parka and stocking cap?

You pushed it too hard on those double-black-diamond slopes. You can hardly stand up straight. What were you thinking? You're going to need a good chiropractor. At the chiropractor's, you decide to purchase a one-month package that includes unlimited visits for $99.96. If you use 6 visits in one month, what will one visit cost?

Teacher Notes—A Guide to Multistep Problem Solutions

Cost of Gasoline:

220 miles / 18.7 mpg = 11.76 gallons.

11.76 gallons × $2.37 = $27.87 spent on gas.

Lift Ticket Price After Discount:

2 × $135.00 = $270.00 for two lift tickets.

$270.00 × .20 = $54.00 discount.

$270.00 − $54.00 = $216.00 total cost after the discount.

Ski Rental Package With Insurance:

$17.56 + $18.14 = $35.70 for the two ski packages.

Insurance is 10% more. Find 10% by moving the decimal one place to the left.

$35.70 + $3.57 Insurance = $39.27 total cost of two rentals with insurance.

Cost for Food and Coffee:

$33.66 × .5 or ½ or divided by 2 = $16.83. Emphasize the relationship between 50%, ½, and any number that is divided by two.

$16.83 + $6.17 + $7.77 = $30.77 for food.

The Parka and Cap After Discount:

$149.00 × .15 = $22.35 for the price of the cap.

$149.00 + $22.35 = $171.35 for the parka and the cap.

Chiropractic Care:

$99.96 / 6 = $16.66 for one visit to the chiropractor.

Breckenridge Ski Trip Tally Sheet

Cost of Gasoline to Breckenridge and Back	$
Cost of Two Lift Tickets Including Discount	$
Cost of Two Ski Rentals with Insurance	$
Cost of Lunch, Coffee, and Dinner	$
Cost of Parka and Stocking Cap	$
Cost of One Visit to Chiropractor	$

Total Cost

Cash Available from Cogwheel Spins

Balance Placed on Credit Card

Lesson 2.7 It Adds Up! Unpaid Credit Card Balances

Having fallen short of the needed cash during a ski trip to Breckenridge, students will calculate the financial effect of unpaid credit card balances.

Materials

◆ Handout: "It Adds Up! Unpaid Credit Card Balances"

Estimated Time

30–40 minutes

Procedure

Distribute the handout "It Adds Up! Unpaid Credit Card Balances."

Allow use of calculators again. Students will get more practice working with percentages, but the larger lesson involves the ramifications of decisions concerning personal finances. Wow! Those credit card fees really add up on unpaid balances!

The calculations here get a bit tedious and repetitive, but this repetition is driving home a very important financial understanding—although, admittedly, a simplified version of it. We've created a lesson in economics, and it's a stronger lesson because the students have produced the calculations applied to the lesson.

Quick mini-lesson: What is interest? Let's let Investopedia explain.

Interest Definition—Investopedia

www.investopedia.com › Investing › Investing Essentials

Nov 25, 2020—Interest is the monetary charge for the privilege of borrowing money, typically expressed as an annual percentage rate (APR). Interest is the amount of money a lender or financial institution receives for lending out money.

Help students put a definition of *interest* in their own words. For example, a student agrees to loan another a candy bar. In return, the student agrees to pay back one candy bar plus two sticks of gum if the candy bar is not paid back by the end of the week.

An answer key to the handout is provided later.

It Adds Up! Unpaid Credit Card Balances

Let's see what would happen to the balance charged on a credit card if no payments were made for one full year—interest compounded each month:

**Balance Charged to Credit Card From Ski Trip—Your Balance at the Beginning of the First Month

Always round to the nearest 100th.

Balance at Beginning of Month	+18% Interest on Balance	= Balance at End of Month
**Month 1		
Month 2		
Month 3		
Month 4		
Month 5		
Month 6		
Month 7		
Month 8		
Month 9		
Month 10		
Month 11		
Month 12		

Think about it: What is one good thing about having a credit card?

Think about it: Why do so many people have unpaid balances on their credit cards?

Balance at Beginning of Month	+18% Interest Added	= Balance at End of Month
Month 1 $200.00	$36.00	$236.00
Month 2 236.00	42.48	278.48
Month 3 278.48	50.13	328.61
Month 4 328.61	59.15	387.76
Month 5 387.76	69.80	457.56
Month 6 457.56	82.36	539.92
Month 7 539.92	97.19	637.11
Month 8 637.11	114.70	751.81
Month 9 751.81	135.33	887.14
Month 10 887.14	159.69	1,046.83
Month 11 1,046.83	188.43	1,235.26
Month 12 1,235.26	222.35	$1,457.61

Teacher Notes: Sample for calculations for interest compounded monthly for $200 placed on the credit card after the ski trip. This is most certainly a simplified version of interest calculations for an actual credit card with an 18% APR. The most important point is an economic one: You pay more the longer you do not pay your balance, and this figure compounds.

Lesson 2.8 Graphic Design and Geometry: The Credit Card Advertisement

The next lesson is another applied graphic design challenge that will further reinforce an economic understanding of compound interest. In this lesson, students view credit card offers that can be found online and use similar language while creating an advertisement for a new credit card.

Materials

- ◆ Handout: "Credit Card Advertisement Graphic Design Challenge"
- ◆ Markers and colored pencils
- ◆ Construct paper of various colors
- ◆ Other craft tools and supplies like glue and scissors, optional

Estimated Time

40–60 minutes

Procedure

Creating the advertisement is an excellent critical thinking exercise—especially as students create titles and catchphrases to go along with the ads. The graphic design of the advertisement takes critical thought as well. What colors will be effective? How should the ad be laid out? Should I include a background picture?

Let's add to the challenge by requiring students to solve little geometry puzzles to be able to draw the credit card accurately. Puzzle solutions: The credit card is 3″ × 5″, and the hologram is 1″ square.

From the Common Core

CCSS.Math.Content.4.MD.A.2
Use the four operations to solve word problems involving distances, intervals of time, liquid volumes, masses of objects, and money, including problems involving simple fractions or decimals, and problems that require expressing measurements given in a larger unit in terms of a smaller unit. Represent measurement quantities using diagrams such as number line diagrams that feature a measurement scale.

CCSS.Math.Content.4.MD.A.3
Apply the area and perimeter formulas for rectangles in real-world and mathematical problems.

Credit Card Advertisement Graphic Design Challenge

Your assignment is to create an advertisement for a new credit card issued by a bank in the Pikes Peak area of Colorado. The credit card will be offered with a 15% interest rate, compounded each month on any unpaid balances. Find advertisements for credit cards online for samples.

- ◆ Come up with a fitting name for the credit card that will attract customers. The name should be related to mountains or Colorado in some way. Include the name in the advertisement.
- ◆ The ad needs to have an eye-catching phrase for the title. Make the lettering for the title clear and attractive.
- ◆ The ad should have a clear disclosure statement. In other words, you must explain the interest rate on unpaid balances.
- ◆ You can include any pictures that will attract customers. This is an advertisement which can be posted on a website or used as printed mailers or in a magazine, and it needs to stand out.
- ◆ The advertisement must include a large image of the credit card. You decide on the background colors or pictures on the card. The design and look of the card will attract people.
- ◆ Draw the credit card to these specifications:

  - It is a perfect rectangle (but draw in rounded corners later to make it look more realistic).
  - The rectangle is formed by two right triangles, each with an area of 7.5 inches^2
  - The base of the right triangles (in number of inches) equals one-fourth of twenty.
  - The rectangle is in landscape orientation.
  - There is a hologram on the top right corner of the credit card that is a square. The hologram measures 1/144th of a square foot.

THE AMBER WAVES CARD FROM ROCKY MOUNT FINANCING:

AMBER WAVES

837 444 228 0639

BYRON WHITE

VISTA

EXPIRES
05/21

"SECURITY AND TRUST - AS STRONG AS THE ROCKIES"

- 19.99% APR FIXED** ON UNPAID BALANCES
- NO ANNUAL FEE

CASH* BACK ON EVERY PURCHASE

* zero balance required

** AVERAGE DAILY BAL. COMPOUNDED ANNUALLY

YOU'LL BE SWAYING IN OPEN FIELDS

Lesson 2.9 Spinner Games

Our students have had to be resilient, persistent, and dedicated to this project to make it this far, and now they will have a chance to have fun with what they've learned in a creative way. They've gone far beyond their classmates working at grade level, and in some cases, they've had to fill in a gap here or there in the standard curriculum—adding to their workloads. That's why we take a couple hours to reward ourselves by creating and playing a game with the spinners we've made.

Materials

- ◆ Handout: "Cog Spinner Game," instructions and rubric
- ◆ Craft supplies

Estimated Time

At least one class period to create the game, and one class period to share the game with classmates, or 1 to 2 hours

Procedure

Distribute the handout "Cog Spinner" for instructions and a scoring rubric.

Of course it's not all fun and games. Designing a good game takes creativity, critical thinking, and application of one's knowledge. That said, we keep the rubric fairly simple (see the following student handout). Notice, however, that part of the rubric requires students use a required skill from the state or local math standards!

Here is also an opportunity to mesh the language arts and math worlds together with the written directions. We want other students to be able to play the game based on written directions. The game might be added to one of your class's math centers and become a more permanent part of your classroom.

From the Common Core

CCSS.Ela-Literacy.W.5.2
Write informative/explanatory texts to examine a topic and convey ideas and information clearly.

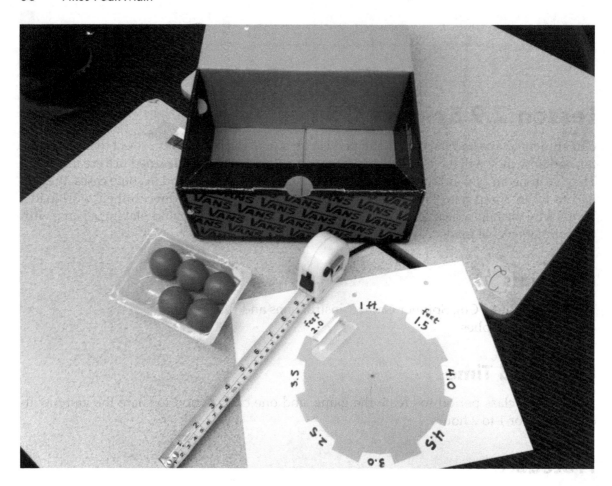

The preceding is an example of an effective game based on the scoring rubric—very playable, using math concepts, and requiring two or more players. Spin the spinner to determine a decimal distance from the shoebox. Measure the distance and attempt to bounce a ping pong ball into the box. Record the results. The highest percentage successful after 10 to 15 spins wins.

Cog Spinner Game

Create a game using the cog spinner you've made. You can place any value into the blank spaces around the cogwheel. Be creative and don't limit your imagination. What would be fun for yourself and others?

Since this is a part of math class, it's important your game involve calculations, but beyond that, it's up to you to decide. Maybe you'll want a required skill like that used in a carnival game. Do you need a playing board? How about cards to draw from a stack? Perhaps your game could be based on a sport or an activity you enjoy. You may have to create other playing pieces aside from the spinner.

There are only two parts to the evaluation rubric for the game, so you have few limits. It's almost wide open! Start by researching the standards for your grade level.

All that said . . . don't make this too complicated. You want other students to be able to figure out how to play the game quickly and have fun so they will want to play it again and again. The best games may become permanent parts of your classroom.

Advanced	Proficient	In Progress
The game requires participants to make math calculations based on grade-level standards or above, and the calculations are an important part of the game. The game's designer has listed the standard.	The game requires participants to make math calculations based on grade-level standards or above, but the calculations are not very important to playing the game successfully.	The game requires participants to make math calculations, but the calculations are below grade level.
Written directions are clear. A student could play the game on their own because they understand what needs to be done.	Directions are clear, but someone must make them clearer through an explanation.	The directions seem confusing or incomplete.

Math Standard Used for the Game:

Lesson 2.10 Geometry Drafting Challenge

In this lesson, students will use scale, geometry, and drawing tools to render representations of an actual blueprint of a ski lift wheel.

Materials

- Handout: "Geometry Drafting Challenge"
- Handout: "Roll-Back Dog Detail"
- Compass and ruler
- Items commonly found in a classroom like tape, books, chairs, and pencils

Estimated Time

30–40 minutes

Procedure

Distribute the handout "Geometry Drafting Challenge."

In the following drafting challenge, students won't so much be interpreting blueprints as creating and managing "scale" for circles. Scale is a seventh-grade Common Core standard. We want the students to use a compass accurately and transform the drawing into a true circle drawn to a smaller scale. Students will not only have to understand scale (ratios and proportions), they'll also need to know center points, radius, circumference, and area for a circle.

Students will further show their understanding of scale by creating their own scale and completing a second drawing—adding circumference and scale for this drawing as well. It sounds complicated, but keep in mind that we're trying to find appropriate challenge for advanced fifth graders. Much of the math in this challenge is actually quite intuitive.

More hands-on geometry follows as students show the actual 10' diameter of the cogwheel in the classroom. Note that the students should also show the wheel's center point—another way to reinforce the geometric components of a circle.

Solutions

- The 1 foot = ½ inch–scaled circle will have a diameter of 6 inches.
- The circumference of the 10' wheel is 31.4 feet; the area is 78.5 square feet.
- Answers will vary for the scale the students have created for the model. Remember that circumference of a circle is $\pi \times$ diameter or $\pi \times 2 \times$ radius. The area of a circle is $A = \pi r^2$.

From the Common Core

CCSS.Math.Content.7.G.A.1
Solve problems involving scale drawings of geometric figures, including computing actual lengths and areas from a scale drawing and reproducing a scale drawing at a different scale.

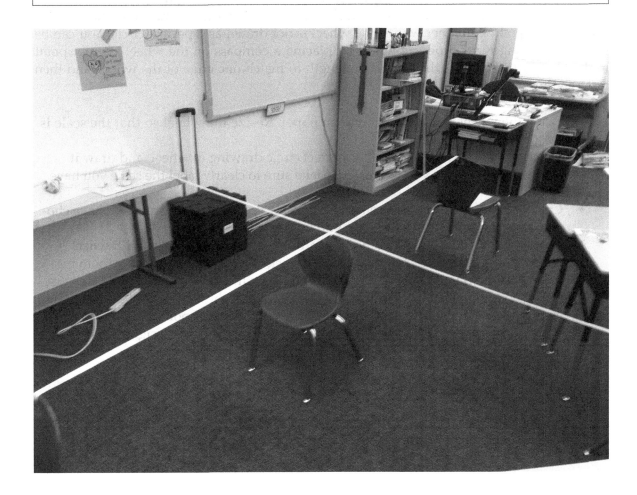

An effective representation of the ski cogwheel is shown earlier with diameters taped across a chair center point. This model made the size of the cogwheel clear to everyone.

Geometry Drafting Challenge

The following is a blueprint for a cogwheel, a "Roll-Back Dog," which is a part of a ski lift. Can you find the label that states the wheel is 10 feet in diameter? Notice that the wheel is drawn in *perspective*. In other words, the wheel is not drawn as a perfect circle. You can be sure the drawing is not a perfect wheel by placing a compass on the wheel's center point in the blueprint, adjusting the compass's length to match one edge of the wheel, and then rotating the compass.

- Draw the wheel as a perfect circle on paper. Resize the wheel so that the scale is 1 foot = 1/2 inch.
- Create your own scale for another perfect circle drawing of wheel, and draw it again using the scale you've created. Make sure to clearly label the scale you have chosen.
- Calculate the actual circumference and area for the circle in the scale you have chosen, and label these in the drawing you've created.
- Calculate the actual circumference and area of the Roll-Back Dog ski lift wheel.
- Show the actual diameter/size of the Roll-Back Dog wheel in your classroom by setting out marking points of your choosing. Your marking points might be chairs, tape, books, or pencils—anything that can be used to show the actual diameter and circumference of the Roll-Back Dog wheel. Mark the center point as well. Note: Do not disrupt others in your class who may be working on other assignments as you are completing this part of the challenge.

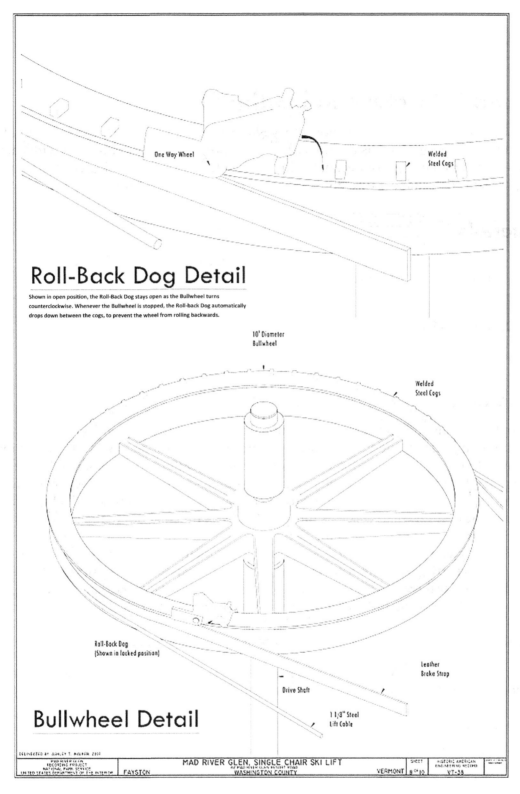

Roll-Back Dog Detail

One Way Wheel

Welded
Steel Cogs

Shown in open position, the Roll-Back Dog stays open as the Bullwheel turns
counterclockwise. Whenever the Bullwheel is stopped, the Roll-back Dog automatically
drops down between the cogs, to prevent the wheel from rolling backwards.

10' Diameter
Bullwheel

Welded
Steel Cogs

Bullwheel Detail

Roll-Back Dog
(Shown in locked position)

Leather
Brake Strap

Drive Shaft

1 1/8" Steel
Lift Cable

MAD RIVER GLEN, SINGLE CHAIR SKI LIFT
FAYSTON   WASHINGTON COUNTY   VERMONT

Source: United States Library of Congress Prints and Photographs Online www.loc.gov/pictures/item/vt0134.sheet.
00008a/

Lesson 2.11 How Tall Is the Skier?

In this lesson, students make yet another calculation in scale by analyzing the height of ski-ers in a vintage poster. This is a multistep scaling/proportion/ratio problem with calcula-tions required to the tenth of decimal values. Using only a ruler and logical-mathematical skills, students determine the height of a skier from a vintage ski poster.

Materials

- ◆ Handout of the vintage ski poster "Winter Sports, National and State Parks"
- ◆ Ruler with both centimeters and inches

Estimated Time

20 minutes

Procedure

Distribute the handout "Winter Sports, National and State Parks."

You might notice students are working more difficult problems with less direction as we move along . . . continuing here with sixth- and seventh-grade standards. I have often allowed the students to use calculators during this unit—especially after they show me that they know how to make a calculation with pencil and paper. I recommend letting students use a calculator in this final task—as this problem is as much about mathematical thinking with scale and proportion as anything else.

Students will not only have to develop and apply their own scale to solve this problem, but they'll have to convert metric to feet and inches if they use a centimeter ruler to measure the male skier. Furthermore, they'll need to convert within a measurement system to trans-form a decimal to feet and inches. Students will also need to make calculations with decimals.

Solutions

As sizes will vary slightly once the image of the skiers is copied, let's assume for a sample solution that the male skier is 18.3 centimeters tall.

18.3 (male skier) centimeters = 6.0 feet.

18.3 / 6.0 = 3.05; therefore 1 foot = 3.05 centimeters.

Female skier = 16.4 centimeters.

16.4 / 3.05 = 5.37 (rounded) feet.

1 foot = 12 inches.

12 × .37 feet = 4.44 inches

The female skier is 5 feet 4½ inches tall.

Check your answer. Does that comparison—6 feet tall to 5 feet 4½ inches—*look* about right to your eye? Yes!

From the Common Core

CCSS.Math.Content.7.G.A.1
Solve problems involving scale drawings of geometric figures, including computing actual lengths and areas from a scale drawing and reproducing a scale drawing at a different scale.

CCSS.Math.Content.6.NS.B.3
Fluently add, subtract, multiply, and divide multi-digit decimals using the standard algorithm for each operation.

How Tall Is the Skier?

Use the vintage ski poster below. Assuming the man is exactly 6 feet tall, how tall—to the nearest feet and inches—is the woman? Use appropriate measurement tools. Tip: think metric and then convert!

Source: United State Library of Congress Prints and Photographs Online: www.loc.gov/pictures/item/92513828/

Wrapping Up the Unit

The collection of student products in a portfolio will be a source of pride in an accomplishment. Save the portfolios of students' work as examples for future students, to share in parent–teacher conferences, or to display during an open house. Along the way, display some of the best work in the hallway or inside your classroom as well.

Bonus Extension

Challenge students to choose a topic they love and create a math challenge based on that topic—much like the math challenges they've been faced with in Pikes Peak Math. Share the challenge they've created with a partner or place it in a math center.

Baseball Field Landscape Architects

Background

As employees of the fictional Teton Mountain Landscape Architecture Company, our students will apply math skills in a real-world task. As a landscape architect, can your students design a baseball field model for the fictional Cheyenne Wind professional baseball team? Can students triangulate the distances of launched baseballs? Find out in this *real-life* applied mathematics challenge, and practice from a long list of core standards.

Several presentation options in the lesson allow the teacher to choose the difficulty of the task—making this lesson appropriate from advanced fourth-grade skills through eighth grade. Whether it be basic measurement to scaling to the Pythagorean theorem, your students will find this applied math task interesting and challenging.

Unit Objective

The student will:

- Use calculations, geometry, measurement, and graphic design to construct an accurate scale model of a baseball field.
- Apply geometry calculations to triangulate distances.
- Apply mathematical scale to create and use models.

DOI: 10.4324/9781003257646-4

Active Core Math Standards

CCSS.Math.Content.4.MD.A.2 Use the four operations to solve word problems involving distances, intervals of time, liquid volumes, masses of objects, and money, including problems involving simple fractions or decimals, and problems that require expressing measurements given in a larger unit in terms of a smaller unit. Represent measurement quantities using diagrams such as number line diagrams that feature a measurement scale.

CCSS.Math.Content.4.MD.A.3 Apply the area and perimeter formulas for rectangles in real world and mathematical problems. *For example, find the width of a rectangular room given the area of the flooring and the length, by viewing the area formula as a multiplication equation with an unknown factor.*

CCSS.Math.Content.4.MD.C.5a An angle is measured with reference to a circle with its center at the common endpoint of the rays, by considering the fraction of the circular arc between the points where the two rays intersect the circle. An angle that turns through 1/360 of a circle is called a "one-degree angle," and can be used to measure angles.

CCSS.Math.Content.4.MD.C.6 Measure angles in whole-number degrees using a protractor. Sketch angles of specified measure.

CCSS.Math.Content.7.G.A.1 Solve problems involving scale drawings of geometric figures, including computing actual lengths and areas from a scale drawing and reproducing a scale drawing at a different scale.

CCSS.Math.Content.7.G.A.2 Draw (freehand, with ruler and protractor, and with technology) geometric shapes with given conditions. Focus on constructing triangles from three measures of angles or sides, noticing when the conditions determine a unique triangle, more than one triangle, or no triangle.

CCSS.Math.Content.7.G.B.4 Know the formulas for the area and circumference of a circle and use them to solve problems; give an informal derivation of the relationship between the circumference and area of a circle.

CCSS.Math.Content.7.G.B.6 Solve real-world and mathematical problems involving area, volume and surface area of two- and three-dimensional objects composed of triangles, quadrilaterals, polygons, cubes, and right prisms.

CCSS.Math.Content.8.G.B.7 Apply the Pythagorean Theorem to determine unknown side lengths in right triangles in real-world and mathematical problems in two and three dimensions.

Launch

Watch Abbott and Costello's famous "Who's on First" routine. One link follows, but you can find many online versions aside from this one: www.youtube.com/watch?v=nZ5vspsNS1g

My gifted students have loved "Who's on First" over the years. You might be wondering how this routine is going to relate to a math project. It will; however, one of the key components of a launch is student engagement, and your kids will absolutely be engaged with this video. You will enjoy watching the reaction of your students as they "get it." Looks of confusion turn to laughter within the first minute, and the laughter becomes infectious.

Our obvious connection to the project to come is baseball, but let's use the video to generate a deeper discussion about the nature of communication and the nature of mathematics as well. Discuss these questions with the class:

- How do you describe the misunderstanding in "Who's on First?"
- How could the misunderstanding have been avoided? Could a diagram with labels have been useful?
- Explain which you think is more likely to lead to a misunderstanding—words or numbers.
- How might numbers and mathematics lead to misunderstanding?
- Watch an example here as Lou Costello proves that $7 \times 13 = 28$: www.youtube.com/watch?v=lzxVyO6cpos
- Architects use diagrams, numbers, blueprints, and models to explain to others how to build something the architect has envisioned. What steps must an architect take in order to assure there is no confusion?

Explain that in this project in which students will become landscape architects, it is their task to transform a client's vision into an accurate model. Let's keep in mind the important components that will lead to mathematical clarity and understanding!

Lesson 3.1 Constructing a Scale Model of a Baseball Field

In the first lesson, students will use guidelines set forth in a real-world math application to construct an accurate model of a baseball field.

Materials

- Measuring and drawing tools like small plastic T-squares, rulers, string, and compasses
- Two shades of brown construction paper
- "Grass-green poster paper
- String, at least 50" per student
- Glue and scissors

Estimated Time

1.5 to 2 hours or even longer, depending on your students' skill levels

Procedure

Distribute the letter below to the students. The letter will serve as both an introduction to the activity as well as a guide to constructing the model baseball field.

Following are suggested adaptations for a variety of abilities in your classroom.

Most Difficult

Use only the written instructions for the dimensions of the baseball field and depend on the students to find a sample field online as suggested. Monitor and adjust if necessary. While one of the important social-emotional lessons in working with gifted students is to learn grit and resilience when faced with difficult tasks, make yourself available as a guide and advisor throughout this process.

Note: Using the Pythagorean theorem, we find the distance between home plate and second base is 127.28 feet: $a^2 + b^2 = c^2$; 90^2 feet $+ 90^2$ feet $= c^2$; $c^2 = 16{,}200$ ft^2. The square root of $16{,}200 = 127.28$ feet.

More Difficult

Use the graphic diagram of the field. Supply the materials, but don't make suggestions about which tools (i.e., ruler, T-square, compass, string) might be used to best make the field's model. Monitor and advise students, encouraging progress, but redirect students only when frustration is running high. Help students use the Pythagorean theorem to calculate the distance between home plate and second base to locate the pitcher's rubber and construct the pitcher's mound.

Difficult

Use the graphic diagram of the field, but first open a dialogue with the students about what measurement tools they might need. Support executive functioning by suggesting a plan, and remind students about mathematical applications for measurement. Provide suggestions and guidance as students successfully complete each portion of the task. Guide students in the use of the Pythagorean theorem or measurement and scale conversions to find the distance between home plate and second base to locate the pitcher's rubber and construct the pitcher's mound.

Fully Guided

Present each section of the task to the class for discussion—gathering suggestions about how each task might be met. Provide the tools and the formulas which will help students succeed. Begin with a discussion of the scale that shows 10 feet = 1 inch. With guidance, individual students should construct the square base-path portion of the infield first. Next, guide students in finding the location of the pitcher's mound and in making an arc for the back of the infield dirt—demonstrating how this can be done using a length of string of the appropriate length. Move on to the outfield dimensions either using strings cut of the appropriate length or meter sticks and rulers. Make sure the students use the right angles formed by the infield and home plate to keep everything "square" in the outfield. Review the use of a compass, and help students construct the batting area and pitcher's mound circles last. Use measurement and scale conversion with meter sticks to find the distance between home plate and second base to locate the pitcher's rubber and construct the pitcher's mound.

*There are a number of mathematical extensions suggested later after the photos of the fields.

Cheyenne Wind Baseball
4488 Cowboy Joe Drive
Cheyenne, WY 82001

Greetings, Teton Mountain Landscape Architecture,

We are excited to bring Class AA Professional Baseball to the great state of Wyoming! We are pleased to be working with you in our educational programs at area schools as well.

We like the progress you've made on our new ballpark—especially the landscape around the clubhouse and the business offices. As we spoke about earlier, we will need a template for creating bird's-eye-view scale models of our field to take to schools for our baseball math program. Please make the template from colored paper—the kind any student can get at school. We will adapt it to a glossy poster model at a later date.

The models should look a lot like stadium seating charts you see when you order tickets online—only much larger, of course!

I realize you are not directly involved with designing the field itself, so I am including the dimensions of our baseball field for your model. We would like the paper models to be on the scale of 1 inch = 10 feet.

Enclosed you will find all the dimensions.

Thanks, and we look forward to seeing your template.

Sincerely,

Zak Sedgewick
Director of Baseball Relations

Cowboy Field Dimensions   Remember: 10 feet = 1 inch

Infield—All Dirt

- Distance between the bases = 90 feet with all bases at right angles to the next base
- Distance from home plate to pitcher's mound = 3½ feet less than halfway between home plate and second base on a straight line segment diagonal
- Distance from pitcher's mound to the edge of outfield grass = from the center of the pitcher's mound, draw an arc with a radius of 90 feet from the foul line behind third base to the foul line behind first base
- Diameter of the circle (pitcher's mound) around the pitcher's rubber, which is the center point of the circle = 25 feet
- Diameter of the circle around home plate (batting area) in which home plate is the center point of the circle = 40 feet

Outfield—All Grass

- Distance from home plate to left-field foul pole = 340 feet
- Distance from home plate to left center wall (approximately midway between the left-field foul pole and "dead centerfield") = 385 feet
- "Dead centerfield" is the point on the outfield wall that is on a straight line to home plate and bisects the infield. "Dead centerfield" is the farthest point in distance from home plate
- Distance from home plate to wall at the "dead centerfield" point = 405 feet
- Distance from home plate to wall in right center (approximately midway between right-field foul pole and "dead centerfield") = 360 feet
- Distance from home plate to right-field foul pole = 320 feet

For examples of fields, see any Major League team's seating charts online. Search with keywords "Texas Rangers Seating Chart," for example. At this link is a seating chart from the Colorado Rockies:

www.mlb.com/rockies/ballpark/seat-viewer

Cowboy Field Dimensions

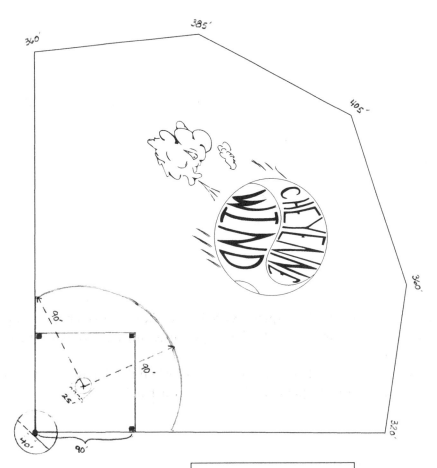

Pitcher's Rubber is 3 ½ feet less than half way from home plate to 2nd base on a straight line.

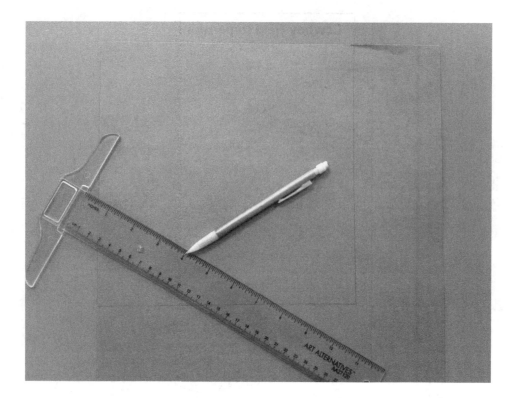

The infield basepaths are a perfect square with 9-foot sides cut from brown paper. Remember that 1 inch = 10 feet in our scale, so the bases (representing a 90-foot distance) are 9 inches apart on our model.

Students who learned how to use a T-square in our Jellyfish Fliers chapter can use one as a quick way to draw a perfect square on the brown construction paper.

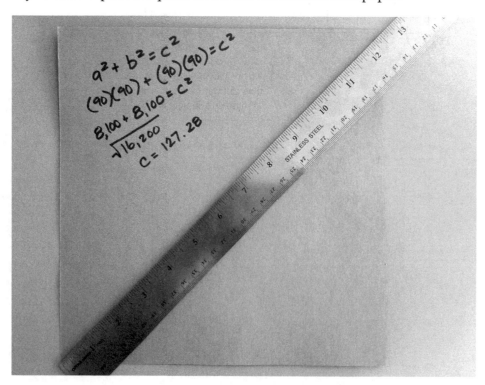

You can help students locate the pitcher's mound either through the Pythagorean theorem (see picture: 127.28/2 minus 3 feet 6 inches = 60 feet 6 inches, or 6½ inches on our scale) or simply by measuring a diagonal on the square infield model. If measurement is used, the pitcher's rubber at the center of the pitcher's mound is located on a diagonal from home plate at approximately the 6½-inch mark.

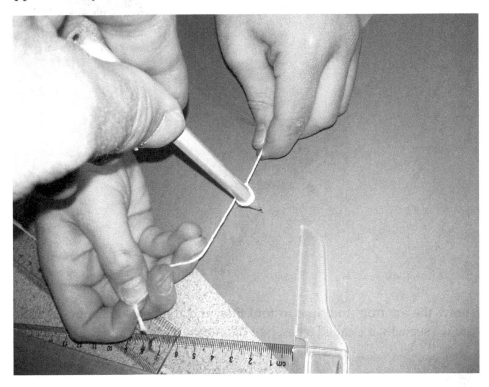

Most of us don't have a compass large enough to draw the arc going around the back of the infield's basepath, so we start by tying a pencil to a string.

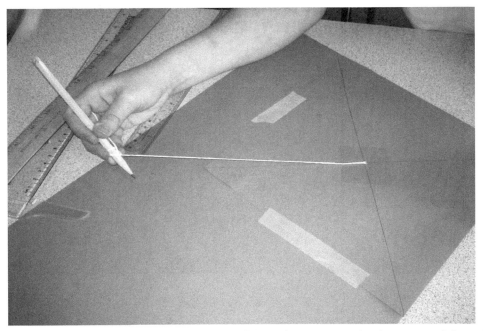

Cut the string to 9 inches (1inch = 10 feet scale) and tape it to the location of the pitcher's mound.

Carefully draw the arc from foul line to foul line, and then cut out your "all brown" dirt infield. Now we see why it's called a baseball diamond!

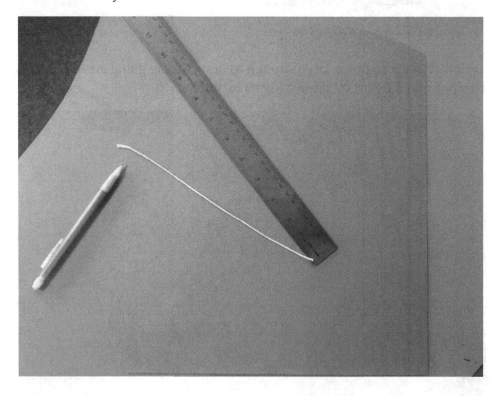

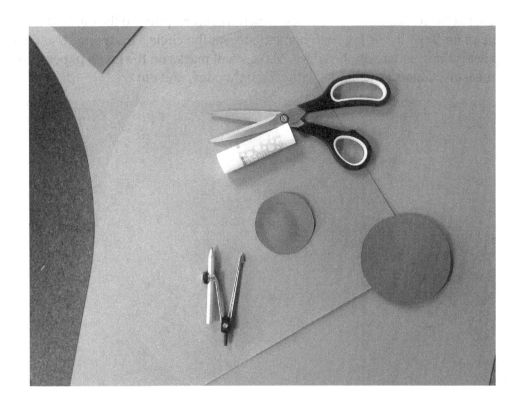

We use a darker brown construction paper to make the pitcher's mound and the batting area. Some students may have a bit of trouble drawing the circles with a compass, but encourage patience. Set the compass at 1¼ inches to draw the circle for the pitcher's mound and at 2 inches to draw the circle for the home-plate area.

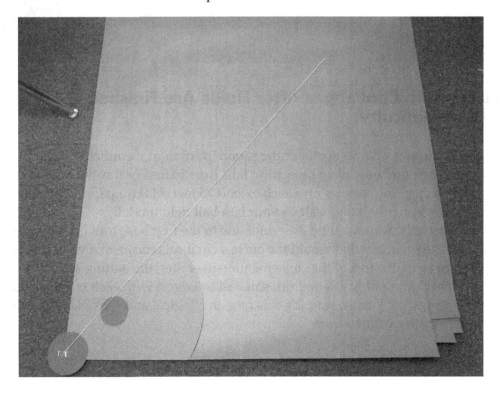

Mark a string at 34, 36, 38.5, and 40.5 inches, which will correspond to the outfield's distances from home plate. Tape the string onto home plate—at the circle's midpoint. Use the infield to line up everything square on the edges. Make small marks on the green paper using your string to measure, connect the marks with a straight edge, and cut.

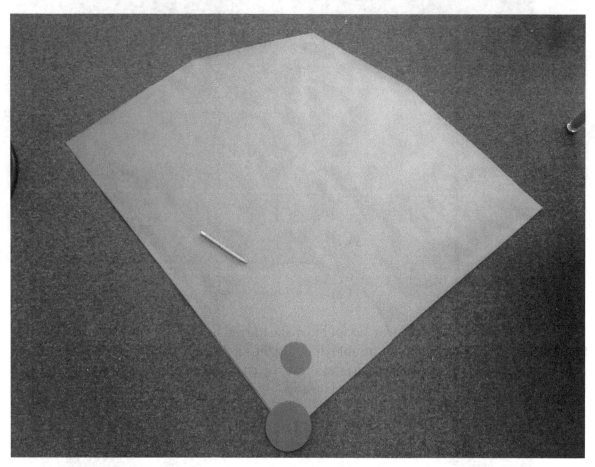

Extension Math Challenges After Fields Are Finished (in order of difficulty)

- ◆ What is the area and perimeter of the square portion of the infield?
- ◆ A screen behind home plate protecting fans from batted or thrown balls is effective in a 45° sector. The sector's rays each extend 75 feet. Make a paper representation of this sector using the same scale as your baseball field model.
- ◆ If the arc made from the third-base foul line to the first base foul line were extended into an entire circle, what would the circle's circumference and area be? Express a comparison of the area of the circle mentioned earlier, the batting area circle, and the pitcher's mound in a ratio from smallest to largest with each number rounded to the nearest 50. Finally, simplify this ratio in a logical and sensible way. Be prepared to justify your answer.

Solutions

♦ What is the area and perimeter of the square portion of the infield?

p = 360 feet   a = 8,100 square feet

♦ A screen behind home plate protecting fans from batted or thrown balls is effective in a 45° sector. The sector's rays each extend 75 feet. Make a paper representation of this sector using the same scale as your baseball field model.

Students should use a protractor to create a 45-degree sector. Each ray will be 7.5 inches in length.

♦ If the arc made from the third base foul line to the first base foul line were extended into an entire circle, what would the circle's circumference and area be? Express a comparison of the area of the circle mentioned earlier, the batting area circle, and the pitcher's mound in a ratio from smallest to largest and each number rounded to the nearest 50. Finally, simplify this ratio in a logical and sensible way. Be prepared to justify your answer.

Circumference = 2(3.14)(90) = 565.2 feet
Area = (3.14)(902) = 25,434 square feet
Pitcher's Mound area = (3.14)(6.252) = 122.66 square feet
Batting Area = (3.14) (102) = 314 square feet
Ratio = 25,450:300:100
One sensible simplification is 255:3:1

Design Extension

Students may want to name their field based on a mascot. A good cross-curricular opportunity exists here as students consider the qualities they'd like their team name to represent and then choose an apt metaphor for the mascot. Students can use the planning sheet below to choose a mascot. Once mascots are chosen, place a picture or name in the outfield grass for your home team—similar to the graphic model seen earlier for the Cheyenne Wind.

What's Your Mascot?

Name_____

Is your team going to be tough and fierce like a bear? But aren't bears known to be sort of lumbering and rough? Maybe your mascot should be some sort of cat? Sleek, quick, intelligent . . . Your mascot doesn't have to be an animal. How about the "turbines" or the "circuit boards" or the "jets"? Shouldn't the name have a nice "ring" to it? Use the graphic organizer below to help explain why you are choosing a particular mascot.

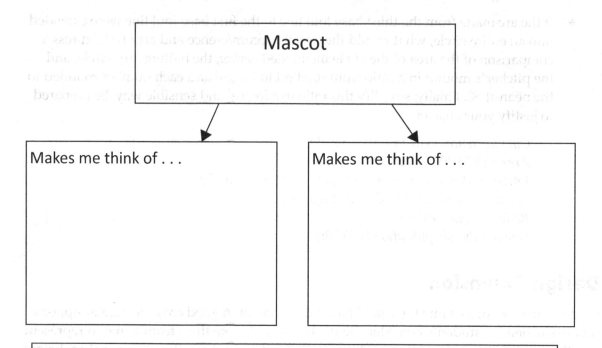

Mascot

Makes me think of . . .

Makes me think of . . .

What are two other animals or things that make you think of the same qualities you listed above?

Consider the possibilities for names. Which is the catchiest, has the nicest ring to it, would be easiest to design a logo for? Write your final choice for a mascot here:

Lesson 3.2 Launch Readings and Triangulation

In this lesson, students make a simple "launcher" to catapult their "baseballs" onto the field. Working in pairs, they'll chart data about their launches and measure the distance by using the Pythagorean theorem. This is sort of a fun way to practice for the older kids and a big mathematical challenge for the younger.

Materials

- Duct tape
- Pencil
- Large paper clip
- Small wooden ball available online or at your local craft store. I bought 50, and they've lasted for years. Alternately, round pieces of cereal or miniature marshmallows may be used. Marbles may work if they are quite small and not too heavy. A little experimentation before the lesson goes a long way
- 50 inches of string per student

Estimated Time

40–60 minutes

Procedure

Constructing the Launcher

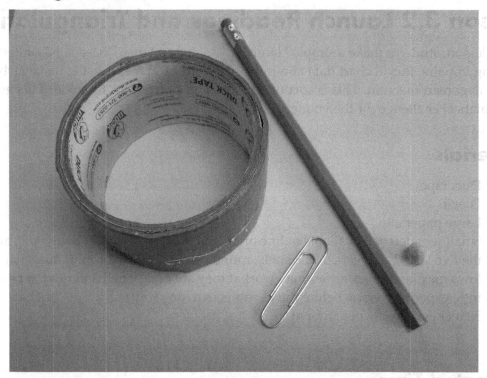

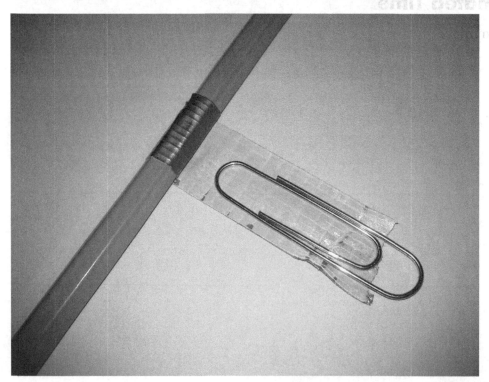

Cut a piece of duct tape about the width of the paper clip and about twice as long as shown earlier. Wrap the duct tape around the middle of the pencil several times. Leave a length of tape that covers most of the paper clip at the end as shown.

Wrap another thin piece of duct tape across the paper clip and tape—sandwiching the paper clip securely in between. The exposed area of the paper clip will cradle the little wooden ball, the round cereal, or the miniature marshmallow.

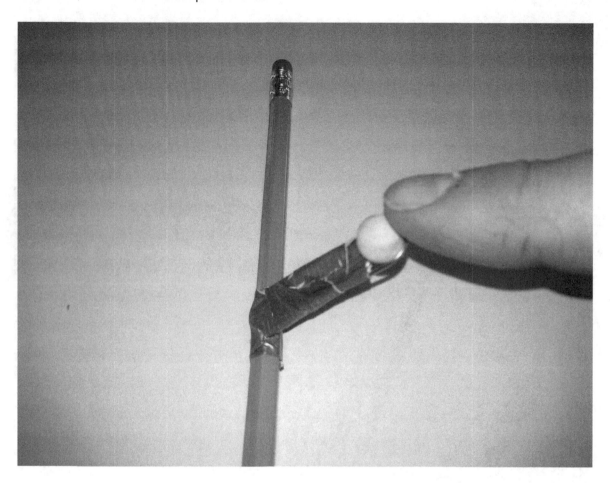

Place the pencil on a flat surface—the paper clip "in front" and sticking up. Mount the wooden ball, round cereal, or mini marshmallow on the launcher. Keep hold of the pencil—not letting it rotate—with one hand while pulling back the paper clip with the index finger of the other. Pull back until you feel tension and then release the launcher. Zing! It's a fly ball to deep left centerfield!

Launch and Triangulate

Now that our launcher is made, we're almost ready to triangulate some distances. First, however, each pair of students will need a 40" string marked at 1" intervals.

Students will use right triangles for this triangulation exercise. I am assuming no teacher using this lesson is working with sine or cosine yet . . . if so, I guess you'll want to consider adapting the lesson to fit trigonometry applications—not unimaginable for upper elementary students gifted in mathematics.

First, one partner of a pair tapes their marked string on a straight line between home plate and dead centerfield.

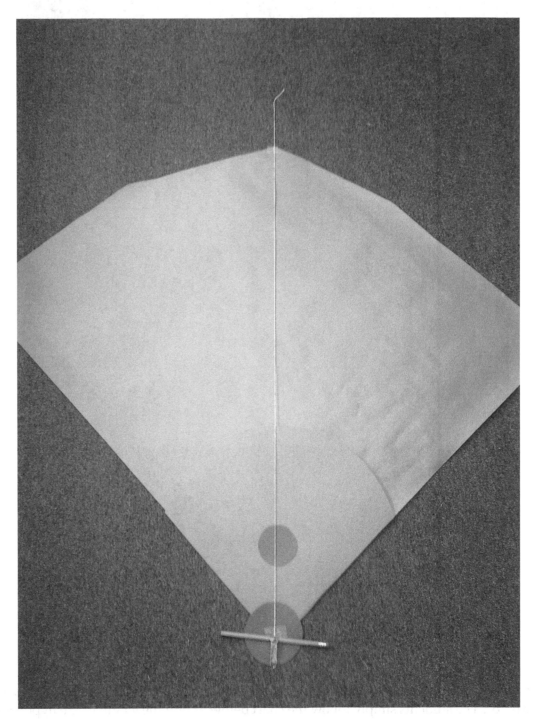

The second partner of the pair launches the baseball from home plate. Our only rule is that the ball must land somewhere on the field. The first person quickly marks where the ball lands and then stretches the second string at a 90-degree angle perpendicular from the center string to where the ball landed—forming two sides of a right triangle. Our only missing side of the triangle is the hypotenuse segment from home plate to where the ball landed, and this hypotenuse also just happens to be the actual distance the ball traveled once it was launched. We'll find this distance using the Pythagorean theorem.

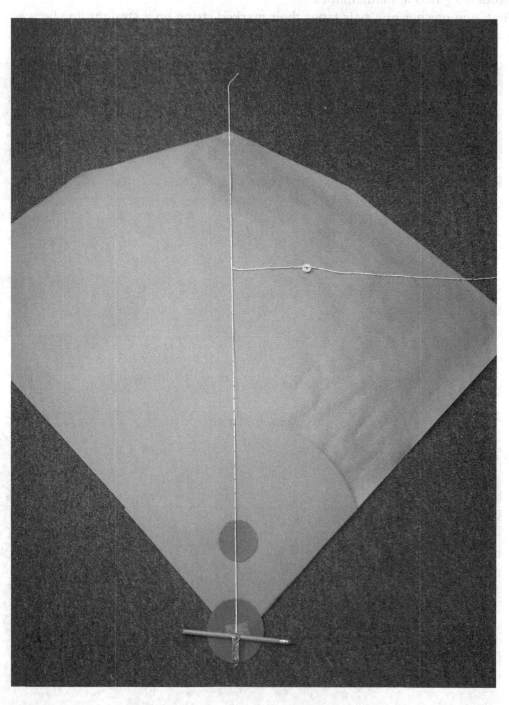

For our purposes, the string between home and center field is triangle side "a"; the string stretched from side "a" to where the ball landed is triangle side "b"; the unknown hypotenuse is "c". The students simply follow the chart below to find the length of the hypotenuse.

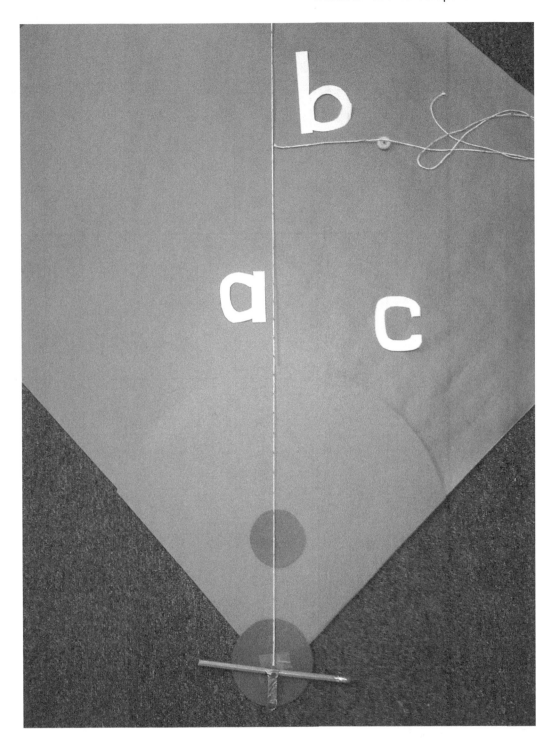

If students have never used the Pythagorean theorem before, have them check their calculations for the distance the baseball flew with one of the marked strings. It can be a cool "Whoa! Math really works in real life!" moment.

Extension

Learn about surveyors and what they do. Explain how a surveyor uses triangulation.

Baseball Launch Triangulation

Name _____

For each launch of the baseball, record the "a" and "b" distances, and estimate the "c" distance in the first three columns. You can make calculations in the last two columns once you're done recording all the launches.

"a" distance to the nearest inch	"b" distance to the nearest inch	Estimate of "c" distance	Calculate (a)(a) + (b)(b) BOX 4	Actual "c" distance = square root of BOX 4

Lesson 3.2 Extensions

- ◆ Invite students to invent a playable baseball game using their fields and launchers.
- ◆ In an extended individual project, challenge students to invent a discus, shot put, or javelin sector and game for a track and field event. A discus might be a button, shots are miniature wooden balls, and javelins could be a toothpick. Young engineers will also need to invent new launching devices!

Cones and Gnome Hat Parachutes

Background

Come on! Who wouldn't want to make a gnome hat parachute? However, it's not so easy the way we will do it. . . .

One of the qualities I like my gifted math students to develop is a willingness to persist in difficult tasks. So many things come easily to them that sometimes they have a tendency to avoid a tough problem.

This quirky, cool three-dimensional drafting and engineering project in which students draw a net for a cone and then construct a three-dimensional cone is not as easy as it seems. It takes grit and precision. It takes careful reading of instructions for a group of kids who are famous for skipping the instructions.

As an independent project, the unit is even more challenging. The directions are written so that the unit may be used as an independent project for students needing more challenge or as a "center" activity in a gifted classroom.

Once the three-dimensional cones have been completed, students may choose optional challenge activities and extend their learning into a real-world STEM challenge—the gnome hat parachute.

As with all the math projects in this book, I urge you to try this out first. The process can get a little confusing, and it helps to know what challenges the students will encounter along the way. Plus, you get to make your very own gnome hat parachute. I bet even your Pinterest friends haven't done that!

Unit Objective

The students will:

◆ Transform two-dimensional geometric nets into three-dimensional constructions.
◆ Precisely draw geometric shapes using drafting tools.

DOI: 10.4324/9781003257646-5

- ◆ Apply the language of the math discipline to understand concepts and accurately apply geometric drawing tasks.
- ◆ Apply geometric calculations with accuracy.
- ◆ Make transformations based on ratios and scale.
- ◆ Make calculations using extended formulas—practicing eliminating like terms as a shortcut.
- ◆ Construct a working prototype.

Active Core Math Standards

CCSS.MATH.CONTENT.6.G.A.1

Find the area of right triangles, other triangles, special quadrilaterals, and polygons by composing into rectangles or decomposing into triangles and other shapes; apply these techniques in the context of solving real-world and mathematical problems.

CCSS.MATH.CONTENT.6.G.A.4

Represent three-dimensional figures using nets made up of rectangles and triangles, and use the nets to find the surface area of these figures. Apply these techniques in the context of solving real-world and mathematical problems.

CCSS.MATH.CONTENT.8.G.B.7

Apply the Pythagorean Theorem to determine unknown side lengths in right triangles in real-world and mathematical problems in two and three dimensions.

CCSS.MATH.CONTENT.8.G.C.9

Know the formulas for the volumes of cones, cylinders, and spheres and use them to solve real-world and mathematical problems.

Launch

Share with the students the animations about cones from the Math is Fun website at www.mathsisfun.com/geometry/cone.html.

As a way of review and to build interest, discuss what you see together:

- ◆ The key components of a cone
- ◆ That a cone is a rotated triangle
- ◆ Right versus oblique cones (note: students will be working with right cones)

- ◆ You may or may not want to work through a couple calculations for a cone's surface area and volume. This will take some time. When we work with this unit, my fifth graders have already made calculations using cones in our regular coursework, so we use the launch as a sort of review and skip any additional calculations.
- ◆ The math fact that a cone is 1/3rd the volume of a cylinder
- ◆ The definition of a *truncated cone*

Invite the students to go on a "cone walk" through the classroom, around the school, and onto the playground. Challenge the students to locate examples of cones or truncated cones. Students will have to look carefully for details. Are there items that are almost but not quite a cone? Keep a list! Report back on the different types of cones, truncated cones, and almost cones that were spotted when students return.

Lesson 4.1 Drawing an Accurate Isosceles Triangle

Students will practice drawing geometric shapes with precision in this first lesson as they draw an isosceles triangle which will become part of the cone net that will be drawn in later lessons.

Material and Tools

◆ Handout: "Designing and Constructing a Three-Dimensional Cone," as well as the "Parts of a Cone Reference"
◆ Ruler and protractor or T-square, one per student

Estimated Time

30 minutes

Procedure

Remember that part of the challenge in this unit is that students are reading and interpreting instructions on their own as much as possible. Your role as a teacher is to advise when necessary, monitor, and encourage students through the process.

Hand out the student instructions, "Designing and Constructing a Three-Dimensional Cone," as well as the "Parts of a Cone Reference." Once students have read through the instructions and studied the parts of a cone, hand out "Isosceles Precision."

Reminders and Details for Teaching This Lesson

1. Students will accurately draw an isosceles triangle which will be the basis for the cone. Students may need to review the properties of an isosceles triangle before they begin.
2. Remind students to use precision in measuring and drawing.

   a. Drawing the line segment which defines the height of the isosceles triangle will be a challenge in itself. We use T-squares in my classroom. In lieu of T-squares, using a ruler and protractor to draw 90-degree angles to the midpoint of the base will be a good challenge.
   b. The cone net that will eventually be drawn derives its measurements from half of the base of the isosceles triangle, the height of the isosceles triangle, and the hypotenuse.

Designing and Constructing a Three-Dimensional Cone

In this lesson, you will begin preparing to draw a two-dimensional plan or a "net" from which you will construct a three-dimensional cone. Be patient. This task is more complex than it might appear in the beginning.

In this lesson, you will

+ draw an accurate isosceles triangle based on a specified size.
+ follow directions closely.
+ draw and design with precision.
+ make careful calculations.
+ first review the parts of a cone.

This page includes important labels for the various parts of a cone. Study it, and then set it aside as a reference as you continue with the work of drawing a two-dimensional cone net.

Parts of a Cone

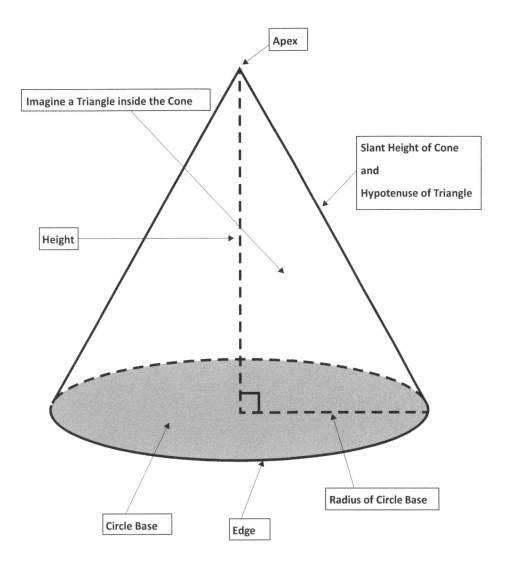

Isosceles Precision

Name_____

Using a ruler or T-square and a protractor, draw an isosceles triangle. The base shall be 10 cm in length. The equivalent sides of the isosceles triangle are of unknown length. The height is 10 cm.

Concentrate on drawing the triangle precisely.

Hint: You will need to find the midpoint of the base. Remember this is an isosceles triangle.

Isosceles Precision

Name_____**SAMPLE**_____

Using a ruler and protractor or a T-square, draw an isosceles triangle. The base shall be 10 cm in length. The equivalent sides of the isosceles triangle are of unknown length. The height is 10 cm.

Concentrate on drawing the triangle precisely.

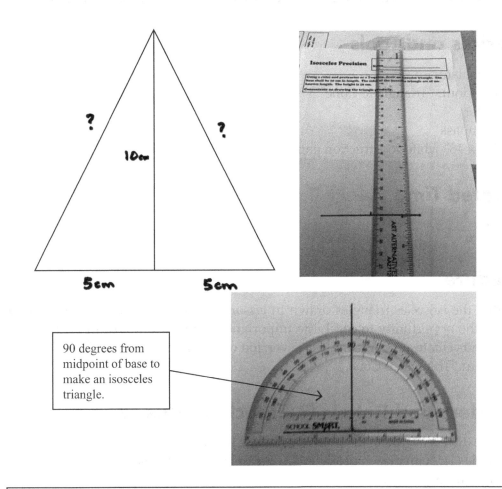

90 degrees from midpoint of base to make an isosceles triangle.

Hint: You will need to find the midpoint of the base.

Lesson 4.2 Triangle to Cone

In this lesson, students begin drawing the cone net. First, students will calculate the unknown length of the hypotenuse of the isosceles triangle they've drawn in lesson 4.1. Next, they'll use this measurement to draw a circle which becomes the circle base of the cone net.

Materials and Tools

+ Calculator
+ Handout: "Triangle to Cone"
+ Ruler
+ Compass
+ 12" × 18" white construction paper

Estimated Time

45 minutes

Procedure

Check that the isosceles triangles drawn in lesson 4.1 are accurately and precisely drawn. Let's take the opportunity to coach the importance of precision in drafting if we need to. Help students create an accurate, precise version of the isosceles triangle if necessary.

Hand out "Triangle to Cone."

Reminders and Details for Teaching This Lesson

1. Use the Pythagorean theorem to calculate the unknown lengths of the isosceles triangle (11.2 cm) drawn in lesson 4.1. We must divide the isosceles triangle into two right triangles to do this.

2. For the calculation, use the height of the triangle as side "b" (10 cm) and one-half of the isosceles base as side "a" (5 cm). Side "c" (unknown length) is the hypotenuse of the right triangle.

   $a^2 + b^2 = c^2$
   $5 \text{ cm}^2 + 10 \text{ cm}^2 = c^2$
   c^2 = the square root of 125 cm = 11.2 cm.

   a. We use calculators to find the square root in my upper elementary classroom. Your students might not—depending on their levels of understanding. As my students are gifted fourth and fifth graders, they are not very well versed in calculating square roots.

3. The measurement for the hypotenuse is quite important. The hypotenuse of the right triangle becomes the basis for the "slant height" of the cone and the radius of the circle base for the cone net—which will be drawn in the second part of the task.

4. When drawing the circle with the 11.2-cm radius, it's helpful to place a couple of extra sheets of paper underneath for extra padding. This is a big circle and not easy to draw. Some students will struggle to draw an accurate circle with a compass. Encourage them to practice. Can they make cool geometric designs while practicing?

Name_____   **Triangle to Cone**

Use the Pythagorean theorem to calculate the unknown length of the isosceles triangle. Round to the nearest 10th of a centimeter. You may use a calculator.

Show your work below. Check your work by measuring the unknown length of the triangle you've drawn in the previous exercise.

Hint: Make sure you use the height of the triangle as part of your calculation.

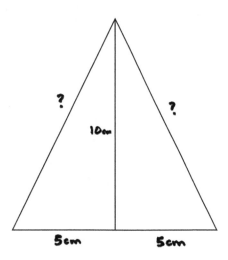

Next, locate a large sheet of white construction paper (at least 12" x 18"). Orient the paper with the long side vertical and the short side horizontal. At the extreme top, left of the paper, draw a circle with a radius equal to the unknown length of the isosceles triangle. A portion of this circle will form the slant height of a cone from its apex to the circular base.

Name__**SAMPLE__A__**

Triangle to Cone

Use the Pythagorean theorem to calculate the unknown length of the isosceles triangle. Round to the nearest 10th of a centimeter. You may use a calculator.

Show your work below. Check your work by measuring the unknown length of the triangle you've drawn in the previous exercise.

$$a^2 + b^2 = c^2$$
$$5^2 + 10^2 = c^2$$
$$25 + 100 = c^2$$
$$c = \sqrt{125}$$
$$c = 11.2 \text{ cm}$$

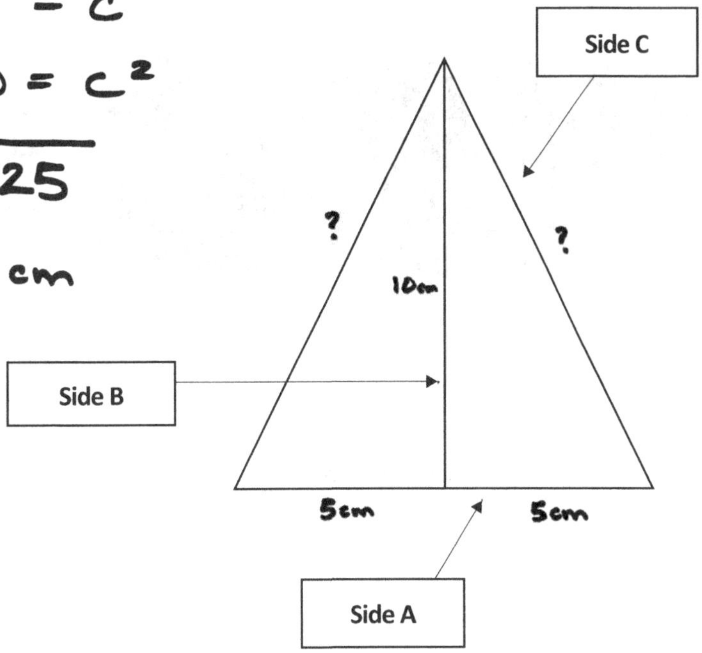

Side C

Side B

?   10cm   ?

5cm   5cm

Side A

Locate a large sheet of white construction paper (at least 12" x 18"). Orient the paper with the long side vertical and the short side horizontal. Near the top of the paper, draw a circle with a radius equal to the unknown length of the isosceles triangle. A portion of this circle will form the upright portion of a cone from its vertex to the base.

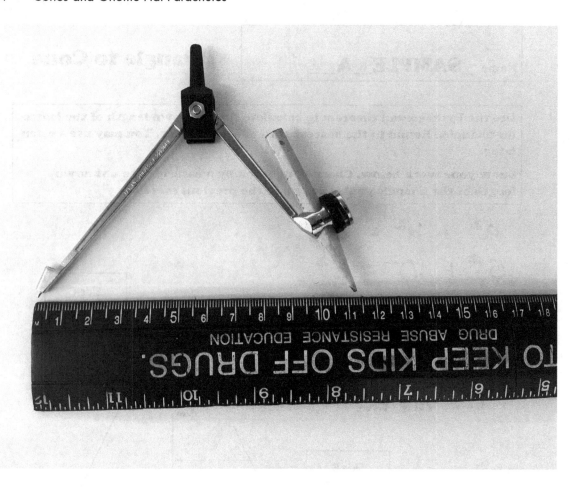

Set a compass at 11.2 cm to draw the circle.

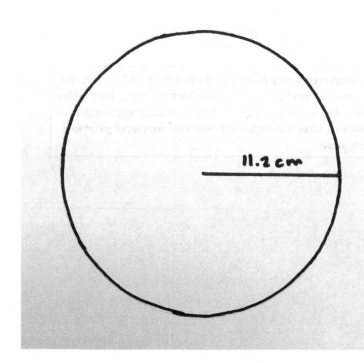

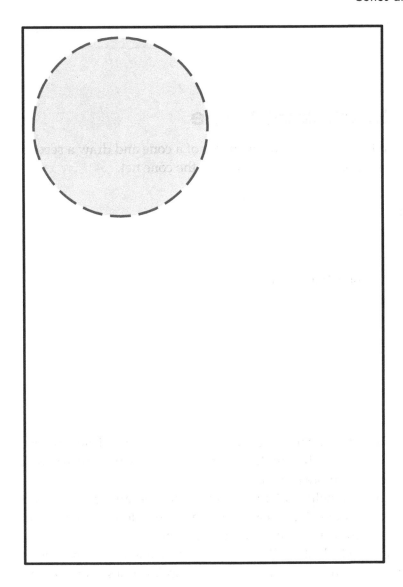

The circle should be drawn at the extreme top, left of the 12" × 18" paper.

The white construction paper should be in the portrait orientation.

Lesson 4.3 Outside Tangent Circle

In this lesson, students will understand visualize the elements of a cone and draw a second circle as an outside tangent to the first on their way to drawing the cone net.

Materials and Tools

◆ Compass
◆ Ruler
◆ Handout: "The Circle in the Cone, Your Cone Net So Far"

Estimated Time

15–20 minutes

Procedure

Check that students have successfully drawn the circle with the 11.2-cm radius from the previous lesson and that the circle is drawn on the top, left of the 12" × 18" white construction paper. If necessary, help students draw a more precise circle.

Distribute "The Circle in the Cone" to help students visualize the emerging cone net and self-check their work thus far. Once students have read through the handout, engage them in a discussion to check for understanding and to clarify any questions.

As per the handout's instructions, students will draw a second circle under the one at the top, left. This circle will derive its radius from the original isosceles triangle (5 cm) and must be drawn as an outside tangent below the first circle. Share the sample shown later to help illustrate. The inside tangent in the sample is for information only and is not a part of the student's drawing.

In order to assess a student's progress and self-check work, hand out the "Your Cone Net So Far" example to students. Encourage students to make any adjustments before continuing to the next lesson.

The Circle in the Cone

Can you find the isosceles triangle inside the cone below? What is the length of the base circle's radius?

On large, white paper, you have already drawn one circle with an 11.2 cm radius. Underneath that circle, draw a second circle the same size as the base of the cone below. Draw this second circle as an outside tangent below the first.

Look up the meaning of *outside tangent* if necessary.

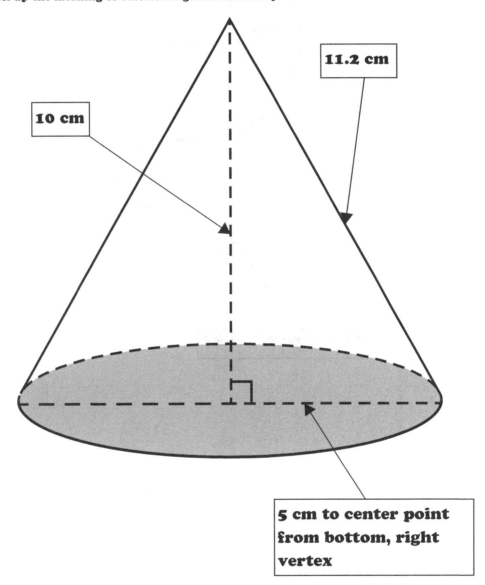

11.2 cm

10 cm

5 cm to center point from bottom, right vertex

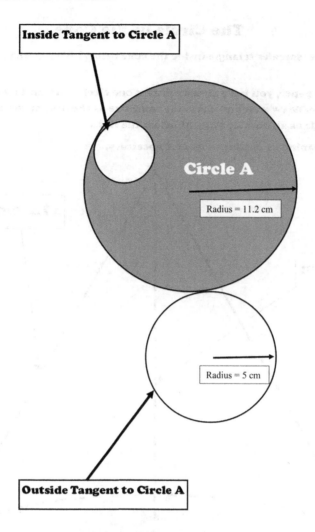

Inside Tangent to Circle A

Circle A

Radius = 11.2 cm

Radius = 5 cm

Outside Tangent to Circle A

Your Cone Net So Far
Checking Your Progress

---

5 cm equals the radius of the base of the cone. 5 cm is also one-half the base of the original isosceles triangle you've drawn. You should have set your compass to 5 cm to draw the second circle.

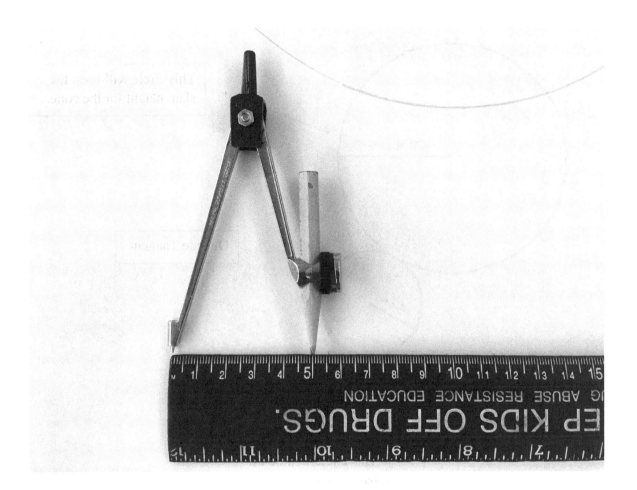

- ◆ You've now drawn the circle which will make up the slant height of the cone from the apex to the base. Refer back to "The Parts of a Cone" if necessary to clarify.
- ◆ You have drawn the circle that forms the base of the cone as a tangent to the larger circle.

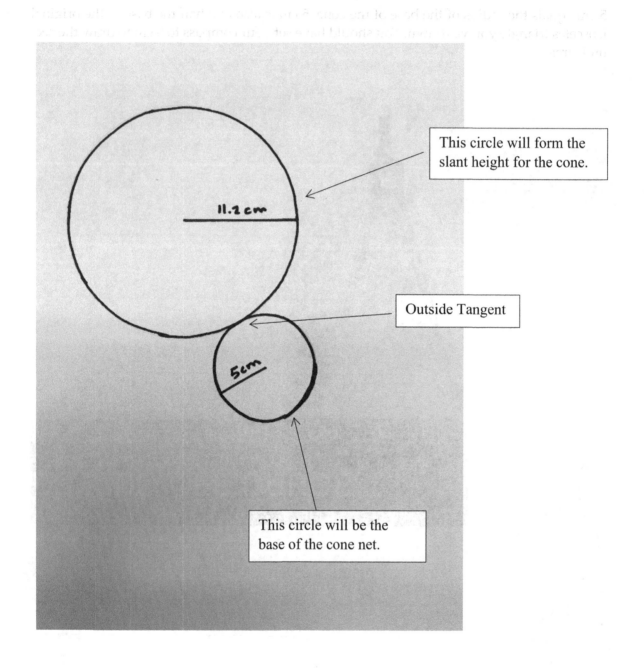

This circle will form the slant height for the cone.

11.2 cm

Outside Tangent

5cm

This circle will be the base of the cone net.

Lesson 4.4 Calculating the Slant Height Section

In this lesson, students will calculate the slant height of the cone by solving an equation. They will gain experience in simplifying an equation in the process.

Materials and Tools

- ◆ Calculator (optional)
- ◆ Handout: "Calculating the Slant Height of the Cone"

Estimated Time

30 minutes

Procedure

It's possible your students will have limited exposure to simplifying equations by eliminating like terms, and this lesson will serve as an introduction to the process. Distribute "Calculating the Slant Height of the Cone." This task will look daunting, but it is actually pretty simple in its execution as we "cross out" like terms in the equation.

The "crossing out" of like terms has been completed in the sample. Only the final calculation is left to the students: 5 × 360 degrees/11.2. The answer is 161 degrees.

Allow students time to reveal this process on their own. Encourage them to read carefully, read, and reread the instructions. This is more excellent practice in patience and resilience for our gifted mathematicians!

A follow-up discussion is imperative. Can students summarize the instructions? Do students understand the process of eliminating like terms in an equation? Let's make sure to talk through this process and solidify understanding. Many students do not encounter the process of eliminating like terms in long equations until high school chemistry or physics. This introduction represents big understandings!

Calculating the Slant Height of the Cone

<u>Review</u>: **Circumference = 2πr (round π to 3.14)**

<u>Remember</u>: **The radius of the small circle is 5 cm. The radius of the large circle is 11.2 cm.**

- **The larger circle with the 11.2 cm radius will form the cone from its apex to the base.**

- **To make this portion of the 3D cone, we will not need the entire circle. We only need a section of the large circle.**

- **We calculate this section by dividing the circumference of the large circle by the circumference of the base circle and then multiply by 360 degrees.**

- **Sound complicated? There is a short cut! (math magic!)**

- **Complete the math magic calculation below to determine the size of the section to form the cone. Some portions have been completed for you already.**

$$\frac{2 \cdot \pi \cdot 5 \text{ cm}}{2 \cdot \pi \cdot 11.2 \text{ cm}} = \frac{\cancel{2 \cdot \pi} \cdot 5 \text{ cm}}{\cancel{2 \cdot \pi} \cdot 11.2 \text{ cm}} = \frac{5}{11.2} \times 360°$$

$$\frac{5 \times 360°}{11.2} = \quad \text{Portion of Circle} \atop \text{Needed (rounded to tenths)} = \boxed{}$$

Sweet! Your answer above is the portion of the large circle you will need to form the slant height of the cone.

Lesson 4.5 Transforming the Net to Three Dimensions

In this lesson, students will remove a section of a circle, practicing precision, and transform a two-dimensional net into a three-dimensional cone.

Materials and Tools

♦ Protractor
♦ Handout: "Final Transformations"

Estimated Time

20–30 minutes

Procedure

Distribute the handout "Final Transformations." Allow students to work through the final stages of transforming the cone net to a three-dimensional cone—supporting or advising when necessary.

Wait a minute . . . have you noticed this cone looks a bit like a garden gnome's hat? Or is it the tip of a giant pencil?

Final Transformations

In the previous lesson, you have calculated the slant height of your cone to be based on a 161-degree sector.

Our next step is to use to create the 161 section from our large circle.

Follow these steps:

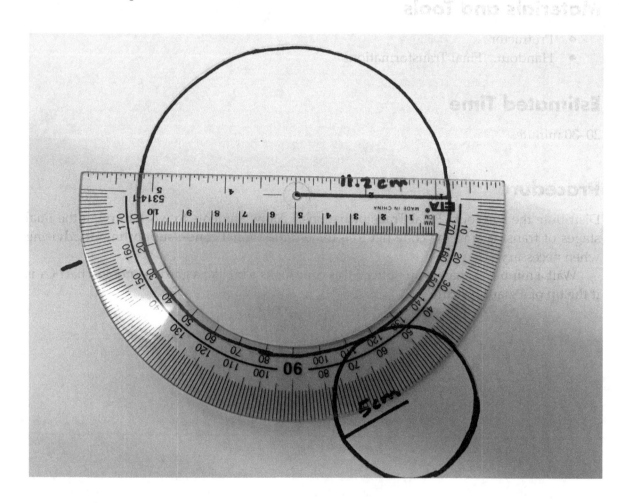

Measure 161 degrees with your protractor (as seen on the left).

Use the straight edge of the protractor to mark a section of the large circle.

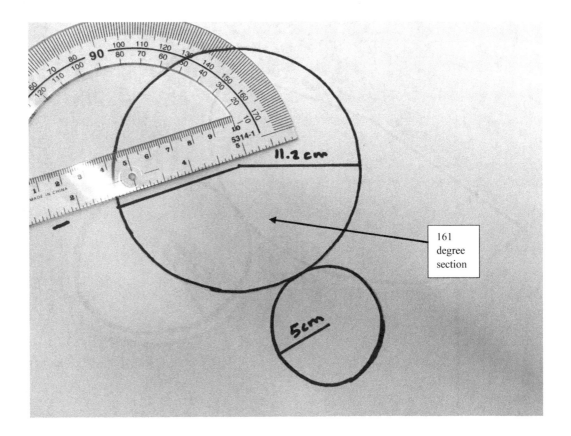

Make sure the 161-degree section is a tangent to the small circle.

- ◆ Your net is finished.
- ◆ Cut it out carefully (right on the lines and not like the one that follows). It's best if you can leave the small circle attached to the 161-degree sector.
- ◆ Trace the net onto another sheet of paper so you have a pattern to use later.
- ◆ Fold and tape the net—transforming it into a three-dimensional cone.

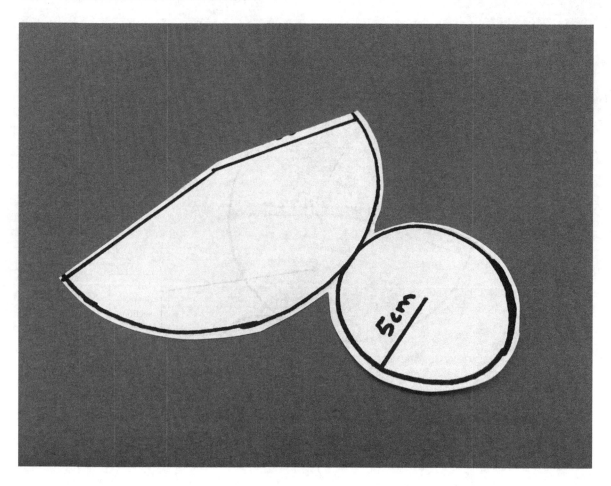

It's OK to separate the pieces, but it's a little harder to tape the cone together that way.

Student Three-Dimensional Graphic Art Challenge (Optional)

In this optional art challenge, students use proportions, ratios, and artistic skills to transform one of their three-dimensional cones into the tip of a giant pencil.

Materials and Tools

- Handout—"*Drawing* on Your Artistic Skills"
- Sharpened pencil
- Cone net
- Meter stick or ruler

Estimated Time

At least 30 minutes, perhaps much longer depending on the student and the artistic decisions made.

Procedure

Distribute the student handout "*Drawing* on Your Artistic Skills." Encourage students to be creative and to construct with mathematical precision at the same time.

Here are some key checkpoints for teachers as you monitor a student's progress:

- The three-dimensional cone is 10 cm in height.
- An actual sharpened pencil's end is approximately 1.5 centimeters.
- The wooden barrel part of the pencil is about 15 centimeters.
- The metal band and the eraser are about 1.5 centimeters.
- The cone is therefore 6.67 times the height of the sharpened end of a real pencil (10 cm/1.5 cm).
- It follows that the barrel of the giant pencil is 100.05 cm or 15 cm × 6.67.
- The giant metal band and the eraser together measure 10 cm or 1.5 cm × 6.67.
- The entire giant pencil is therefore approximately 120 cm in length.

  (Answers will vary slightly depending on the actual pencil used as a model— using a simple proportion to calculate.)

Constructing the pencil portion of the project might be as simple as making the pencil's barrel from rolled-up poster paper. The thickness of the barrel will simply match the thickness of the three-dimensional cone.

Drawing on Your Artistic Skills

Hmmm . . . one of your 3D cones sort of looks like the tip of a pencil. Using measurements of an actual pencil and calculations based on ratios and proportions, can you transform a cone into a giant 3D pencil?

The best 3D products will be both mathematically precise and pleasing works of art.

The student's artwork is excellent in the photo, but are the measurements for the giant pencil accurate?

Gnome Hat Parachutes (optional)

Cones make wonderful gnome hats, and gnome hats on strings make fun little parachutes. In this optional challenge, students meet a real-world engineering challenge by making and testing gnome hat parachute prototypes.

Material and Tools

- ◆ Red construction paper, 11" × 17"
- ◆ Cone net (created in previous lessons)
- ◆ String or yarn
- ◆ Craft sticks, cotton, and glue for the gnome's face
- ◆ Scissors, ruler, and measuring tape
- ◆ Handout: "Gnome Hat Parachute Prototype Challenge"
- ◆ Small assorted "googly eyes" (optional)

Estimated Time

90 minutes or more

Procedure

Distribute the handout "Gnome Hat Parachute Prototype Challenge," and review the contents together with the students.

Let's emphasize a couple physics points to students as we review the instructions for the prototype challenge. First, students are required to hold two constants. The size of the parachute is one constant. The parachute must be made from the three-dimensional cones with the base removed. The second constant is the mass/weight of the gnome passenger attached to the chute. We make these from large craft sticks, cotton, and glue or tape.

Students, however, will adjust two variables. One is the length of the string and placement of the parachute string, which will affect balance. The other variable includes alteration of the cone. Do locations and size of holes cut into the cone parachute enhance flight? Do you need any holes at all?

Encourage the students to make several parachutes and try them out. Choose their best parachute for the trials that will follow. Some examples of how variables have been manipulated by some of my former students, as well as some reference photos and tips, are shown.

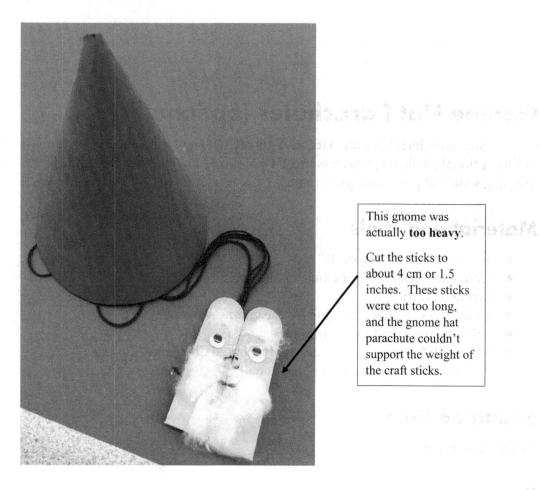

This gnome was actually **too heavy**.

Cut the sticks to about 4 cm or 1.5 inches. These sticks were cut too long, and the gnome hat parachute couldn't support the weight of the craft sticks.

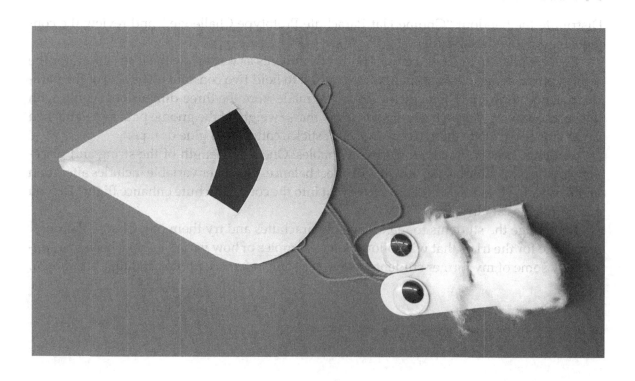

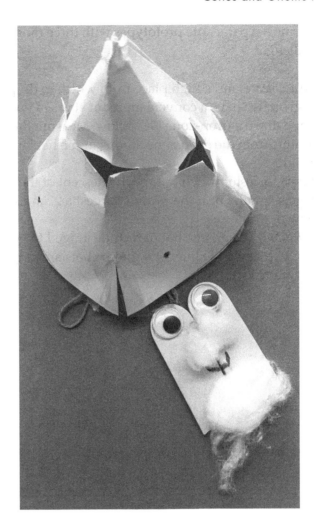

The preceding photos are a couple of the gnome hat parachutes with different designs cut into the parachute. The second example has flaps that can be opened or closed. In this way, the student engineer was able to experiment with the openings without having to make several cones.

We evaluate the gnome hat parachute prototypes with three ratings, and the lowest score wins the prototype challenge.

1. *Drop-Zone Displacement*: Find a high place from which to drop the parachutes—balcony, loft, and so on. We have a convenient set of stairs in our school that we use as a drop zone. Tape down a drop-zone "X" below. Measure the distance the gnome hat parachute lands from the drop zone. Bonus: if the hat lands upright, the distance is cut in half!
2. *Time Aloft Rating*: Use a stopwatch to time the descent of the parachutes. The longest time aloft gets a rating of 1, the second longest a 2, and so on. (Remember, the lowest score wins.)
3. *Coolness Factor Rating*: The gnome hat parachute judged to be the coolest gets a rating of one . . . and on down the line. Our gnome hats are judged by students from another class or grade level.

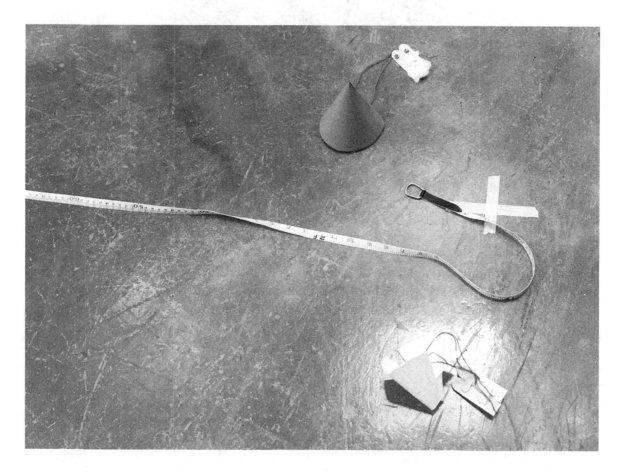

The image shows our drop zone under the stairs with two of the gnome hat parachutes beside it. The parachute at the top of the picture landed "hat up"—gaining the half distance bonus score.

Each student will have their own rating form to be printed (shown later).

Gnome Hat Parachute Prototype Challenge

Have you noticed your three dimensional cone looks like a little gnome hat?

A toy company has noticed this too!

Your challenge is to attach strings and a gnome face to make a gnome hat parachute toy prototype.

Your gnome hat parachute will be evaluated based on three ratings.

Drop Zone Displacement:

How close can you get your parachute to drop to the center of a drop zone?

Time Aloft: The slower the parachute falls, the better. No gnomes may be harmed in this challenge!

Coolness: This toy must sell, and the cooler it is, the more it will sell. Your gnome hat parachute will be judged by a panel of experts.

Things you can adjust for your prototype:

• Length, color, and placement of strings

• Holes cut—different size and placement—in the parachute. Or leave it solid.

• Decoration, color, and appearance of the gnome face.

Things you cannot adjust:

• The weight or mass of the gnome face.

• The size of the cone parachute.

How to make a gnome face which hangs by strings under the parachute hat:

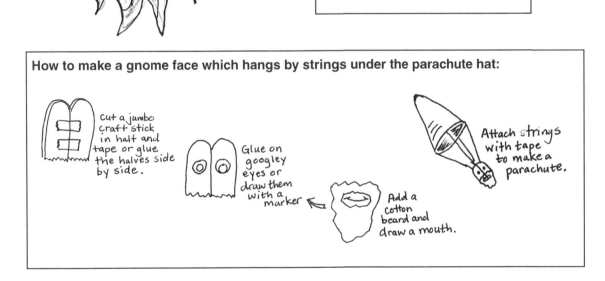

Cut a jumbo craft stick in half and tape or glue the halves side by side.

Glue on googley eyes or draw them with a marker

Add a cotton beard and draw a mouth.

Attach strings with tape to make a parachute.

Gnome Hat Parachute Rating

Drop Zone Distance_____ **Rating** _____

Time Aloft _____ **Rating** _____

Coolness Factor Rank   **Rating** _____

Lowest Score Wins—Total Rating

NAME _____

Judges' Comments:

Unit Follow-Up

Offer to students that in this unit, we have undertaken the engineering design process to generate the best designs. As a class, invite students to describe the engineering design process as they have experienced it. Record and revise the responses together. Use the end product as a classroom poster—reminding students of the effective process for generating solutions to real-world engineering problems.

The process, as described by Teach Engineering (www.teachengineering.org/design/designprocess), is as follows:

1. Ask: Identify the Need & Constraints
2. Research the Problem
3. Imagine: Develop Possible Solutions
4. Plan: Select a Promising Solution
5. Create: Build a Prototype
6. Test and Evaluate Prototype
7. Improve: Redesign as Needed

Gnome Hat Parachute Challenge— Teacher Notes

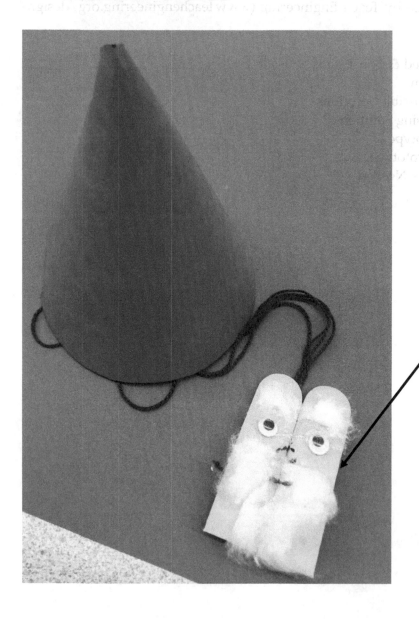

> My gnome was actually **too heavy**.
>
> Cut the sticks to about 4 cm or 1.5 inches.

We've noticed our three-dimensional cones look like little gnome hats, so let's have some fun with it.

In this STEM prototype challenge, students are invited to engineer the most efficient and cool gnome hat parachute.

Students keep two constants. The size of the parachute is one constant. The parachute must be made from the three-dimensional cones with the base removed.

The second constant is the mass/weight of the gnome passenger attached to the chute. We make these from a couple large craft sticks, cotton, and glue/tape. See the following discussion.

Two variables exist. One is the length of the string and placement of the parachute string, which will affect balance.

The other variable includes alteration of the cone. Do locations and size of holes cut into the cone parachute enhance flight? Do you need any holes at all?

Encourage the students to make several parachutes and try them out. Choose their best parachute for the trials.

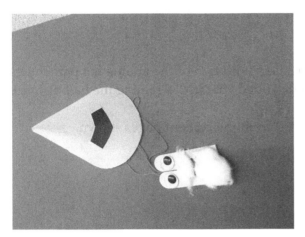 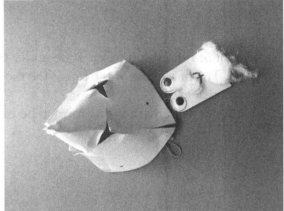

The photos show a couple of the gnome parachutes with different "hole cut" designs. I like how the one on the right has flaps that can be opened or closed. This way the student can experiment with the openings without having to make several cones.

We evaluate the gnome hat parachute prototypes with three ratings—the lowest score wins the prototype challenge.

1. *Drop-Zone Displacement*: Find a high place from which to drop the parachutes—balcony, loft, and the like. We have a convenient set of stairs in our school. Tape down a drop-zone "X" below. Measure the distance the gnome hat parachute lands from the drop zone. Bonus: if the hat lands upright, the distance is cut in half!
2. *Time Aloft Rating*: Use a stopwatch to time the descent of the parachutes. The longest time aloft gets a rating of 1, the second longest a 2, and so on. (Remember, the lowest score wins.)
3. *Coolness Factor Rating*: The gnome hat parachute judged to be the coolest gets a rating of one . . . and on down the line. Our gnome hats are judged by students from another class or grade level.

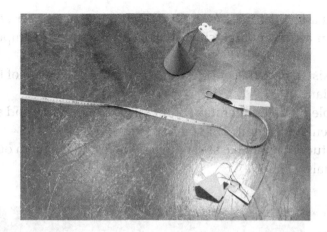

The photo shows our drop zone under the stairs with two of the gnome hat parachutes beside it. The parachute at the top of the picture landed "hat up"—gaining the half distance bonus score.

Students will have a rating form to be printed from the student pages shown.

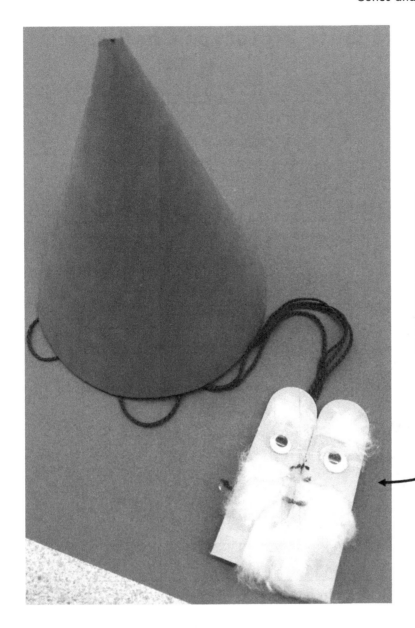

This gnome passenger is too heavy!

Cut your craft sticks about 4 cm or 1 ½ inches long.

Gnome Hat Parachute Prototype Challenge

Have you noticed your three dimensional cone looks like a little gnome hat?

A toy company has noticed this too!

Your challenge is to attach strings and a gnome face to make a gnome hat parachute toy prototype.

Your gnome hat parachute will be evaluated based on three ratings.

Drop Zone Displacement:

How close can you get your parachute to drop to the center of a drop zone?

Time Aloft: The slower the parachute falls, the better. No gnomes may be harmed in this challenge!

Coolness: This toy must sell, and the cooler it is, the more it will sell. Your gnome hat parachute will be judged by a panel of experts.

Things you can adjust for your prototype:

- Length, color, and placement of strings

- Holes cut—different size and placement—in the parachute. Or leave it solid.

- Decoration, color, and appearance of the gnome face.

Things you cannot adjust:

- The weight or mass of the gnome face.
- The size of the cone parachute.

How to make a gnome face which hangs by strings under the parachute hat:

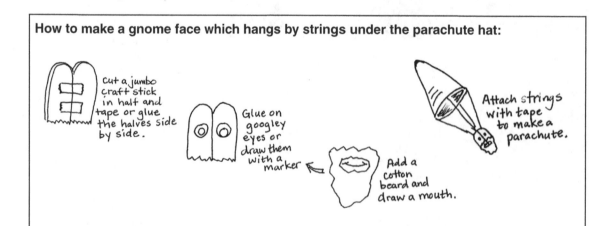

Cut a jumbo craft stick in half and tape or glue the halves side by side.

Glue on googley eyes or draw them with a marker

Add a cotton beard and draw a mouth.

Attach strings with tape to make a parachute.

Gnome Hat Parachute Rating

Drop Zone Distance _____ **Rating** _____

Time Aloft _____ **Rating** _____

Coolness Factor Rank _____   **Rating** _____

Lowest Score Wins—Total Rating

NAME _____

Judges' Comments:

Nametag Math Project

Background

This may be exactly the sort of math challenge you want for your gifted math students who think that school is full of math problems they can zip their way through. It's easy! (Insert evil teacher cackle.) Ha, ha. . . . Nope! It's not now!

This little project takes grit and persistence, creativity, graphic design skills, and math skills. It's real life and hands-on and will take several hours to complete.

My fifth graders wanted this to be a snap. They're used to all this easy stuff, right? It looked cute and fun. Instead, they were scratching their heads as they tried to design the nametags to the exact specifications. They had to organize and interpret as they determined costs. They had to learn new skills. How do you find the area of a trapezoid . . . let alone draw one to specifications? How do you calculate a discount? Pay taxes? You've got to be kidding me! On top of this, they had to keep all the numbers organized and accurate for the accounting. The end result was satisfying, but it wasn't easy getting there.

In this math project, students design desktop nametags to fit specifications, choose from companies that will print the nametags, figure costs, receive "sales" based on their performance on a grading rubric, and then make a tax payment to the U.S. Treasury. Bonus activities further analyze income taxes. And, oh yeah . . . writing mathematically and logically is required!

Unit Objectives

The student will:

- Develop and design physical products based on specifications in a rubric.
- Use applied math to make good business decisions.
- Use geometric formulas and drafting tools to accurately apply geometric figures to a design project.
- Use mathematical logical thinking to defend economic decisions and practices.
- Apply math concepts in a real-world project.

DOI: 10.4324/9781003257646-6

Common Core State Standards focus on base ten fifth-grade decimals and go up through seventh-grade geometry real-world applications.

CCSS.Math.Content.5.NBT.B.7
Understand the place value system.

CCSS.Math.Content.5.NBT.A.1
Recognize that in a multi-digit number, a digit in one place represents 10 times as much as it represents in the place to its right and 1/10 of what it represents in the place to its left.

CCSS.Math.Content.5.NBT.A.2
Explain patterns in the number of zeros of the product when multiplying a number by powers of 10, and explain patterns in the placement of the decimal point when a decimal is multiplied or divided by a power of 10. Use whole-number exponents to denote powers of 10.

CCSS.Math.Content.5.NBT.A.3
Read, write, and compare decimals to thousandths.

CCSS.Math.Content.5.NBT.A.3.a
Read and write decimals to thousandths using base-ten numerals, number names, and expanded form, e.g., $347.392 = 3 \times 100 + 4 \times 10 + 7 \times 1 + 3 \times (1/10) + 9 \times (1/100) + 2 \times (1/1000)$.

CCSS.Math.Content.5.NBT.A.3.b
Compare two decimals to thousandths based on meanings of the digits in each place, using $>$, $=$, and $<$ symbols to record the results of comparisons.

CCSS.Math.Content.5.NBT.A.4
Use place value understanding to round decimals to any place.

Perform operations with multi-digit whole numbers and with decimals to hundredths.

CCSS.Math.Content.5.NBT.B.5
Fluently multiply multi-digit whole numbers using the standard algorithm.

CCSS.Math.Content.5.NBT.B.6
Find whole-number quotients of whole numbers with up to four-digit dividends and two-digit divisors, using strategies based on place value, the properties of operations, and/or the relationship between multiplication and division. Illustrate and explain the calculation by using equations, rectangular arrays, and/or area models.

CCSS.Math.Content.5.NBT.B.7
Add, subtract, multiply, and divide decimals to hundredths, using concrete models or drawings and strategies based on place value, properties of operations, and/or the relationship between addition and subtraction; relate the strategy to a written method and explain the reasoning used.

Solve real-world and mathematical problems involving area, surface area, and volume.

CCSS.Math.Content.6.G.A.1

Find the area of right triangles, other triangles, special quadrilaterals, and polygons by composing into rectangles or decomposing into triangles and other shapes; apply these techniques in the context of solving real-world and mathematical problems.

Draw construct, and describe geometrical figures and describe the relationships between them.

CCSS.Math.Content.7.G.A.1

Solve problems involving scale drawings of geometric figures, including computing actual lengths and areas from a scale drawing and reproducing a scale drawing at a different scale.

CCSS.Math.Content.7.G.A.2

Draw (freehand, with ruler and protractor, and with technology) geometric shapes with given conditions. Focus on constructing triangles from three measures of angles or sides, noticing when the conditions determine a unique triangle, more than one triangle, or no triangle.

Solve real-life and mathematical problems involving angle measure, area, surface area, and volume.

CCSS.Math.Content.7.G.B.4

Know the formulas for the area and circumference of a circle and use them to solve problems; give an informal derivation of the relationship between the circumference and area of a circle.

Launch

View *A Tale of Two Lemonade Stands*, www.youtube.com/watch?v=6JVG3abLBoU. Even if the Nametag Math project is paced individually, I recommend this video as a whole-class critical thinking activity. The short animated advertisement for Chipotle is engaging and generates excellent discussion. It also serves as an intriguing preview for the Nametag Math project.

Once the students have viewed the video, ask one single question: What is this video really about? Answers will vary. Students may suggest the film is about finding love, finding oneself, finding the things that are really important in life, or perhaps how economics can take over a person's life. Regardless of the response, encourage students to explain their viewpoint using details from the video as support.

Now direct the students to think about the economic aspects of the video by asking one additional question: What did the characters do to encourage their lemonade businesses to grow? Answers will vary, but some of the growth was encouraged by advertising, improvements to the stands themselves, offering a variety of menu items, mass production of products, and developing flashy, unique products which may appeal to customers. Students may also mention the passion and dedication of the lemonade stand owners—though ultimately misdirected—as well.

Follow-up the discussion with an introduction to the Nametag Math Project is detailed in the following section.

Introducing the Lesson

The sample dialogue that follows will help teachers introduce the project. After a discussion in which students always end up asking most of the right questions anyway, go over the project requirements and the evaluation rubric.

I suggest introducing the lesson at least a day in advance. Let some ideas rattle around in the back of students' minds for a bit before they begin working on the project.

Sample Dialogue for Introducing the Nametag Project

So you've noticed . . . every year since kindergarten there has been a nametag awaiting you on top of your desk the first day of school. And it's not just you, either. Every kid has one! Does every kid in every school in Canada and the United States have a nametag? That has to be a lot of kids. There have to be gazillions of teachers buying these nametags templates over the summer! Somebody is making a load of money. Shouldn't that someone be you?! Well . . . why not?

In this challenging math project, you will design a nametag pattern to be used in an elementary school classroom. Imagine a teacher browsing through a "teacher" store, looking for the perfect nametags to decorate the tops of students' desks. That teacher will buy a package of 30 nametags, and naturally you prefer those nametags to be of your design. The nametags you design will have to be eye-catching, practical, and neat. They'll need to be colorful, of course. Have you ever known an elementary teacher to decorate in black and white?

This isn't a sidewalk lemonade stand. This is serious business. While designing your nametag, you'll need to keep costs in mind. Every penny that you spend printing the nametags is a penny you don't get to keep in profits. These pennies add up! Fractions of pennies add up, too! Once you've made an excellent design, you will send a print order of 100,000 nametags. Your final design will need to be error-free and well designed when it goes to the print shop, and it must meet the project requirements as well. You'll have a choice of two print services to use. Compare the costs carefully. Errors in math have real-life consequences here. If you want to keep your job, you don't want to waste thousands of dollars choosing the wrong printing company.

Be patient. Try different designs. Use measuring and drawing tools, and make sure to be precise in using them. Use only four or fewer colors. Each different color used will be an added expense when the nametags go to the printer. Use graph paper to try out your ideas and to make calculations. Check your work against the rubric your teacher provides. You'll have to keep trying to make everything work. It's going to take time. You won't race through this one successfully, so be patient. Good luck!

Lesson 5.1 Designing a Nametag

In this lesson, students will design a nametag based on the guidelines set forth in the rubric.

Materials

- Grid paper
- Drafting tools like rulers, compasses, triangles, circle templates, and T-squares
- Handouts: "Desktop Nametag Project Design and Sales Project Guidelines" and "Nametag Rubric"
- Cardstock in a variety of colors

Estimated Time

More than 1 hour and up to several class periods. Students will work at their own pace as they solve math problems and design their nametags. You will notice in larger classes that students will begin to seek out others who are at similar design or calculation stages. Allow this healthy collaboration process to take shape naturally.

Procedure

Distribute the handout "Desktop Nametag Project Design and Sales Project Guidelines" as well as the "Nametag Rubric."

Discuss the requirements of the project as well as the scoring rubric with the students. Make sure students are clear on the larger requirements. As the students work on the nametags, there will be plenty of time to refer back to the specifics set forth in the scoring rubric. Moreover, encourage students to frequently refer back to both the guidelines and the rubric throughout the nametag design process.

Following are some key components to monitor as students work.

Teaching Notes on Nametag Design and Geometry

The following are notes on some of the biggest challenges my fourth and fifth graders experienced.

Persistence is vital and a key social-emotional component for our gifted learners. Students should make drafts of their final product and realize they're not going to bring this all together in one try. Graph paper drafts are very useful in this process. In addition, students need to keep referring back to the rubric so they can meet geometric specifications.

Typically, most teaching and guiding will be for individuals as problems and frustrations arise. Remember, we want students to try to engage with challenges on their own first—maybe fail just a bit, work with frustration, and practice gritty classroom behavior they are so unfamiliar with most of the time. The teacher's job is to gently guide students through frustration and urge students not to give up.

That said, some teachers may prefer to review and teach some important mini-lessons up front.

Using a T-Square

If you have T-squares available, this lesson becomes a neat little exercise in using this handy tool. Students use T-squares to make the nametag itself as well as to draw the three parallel lines for the name on the nametag. Of course, the same results can be made through the use of a ruler. Using a ruler to draw perfect corners and parallel lines is another challenge in itself and actually more difficult than drafting with a T-square. Are the nametag's corners all 90 degrees and each side the proper length? Are the lines for the name of the proper length and parallel? Note: the rubric does not specify the distance between the parallel lines. This decision is part of the graphic design and an important part of the overall appearance of the nametag, however. We want the names on the nametags to be large.

Calculating the Area of a Right Triangle

We had to review this standard. Grab some graph paper. The area of a right triangle = 1/2 base × height. The rubric calls for a right triangle with an area of 6 cm^2. One example of a right triangle with an area of 6 cm^2 is a 4 cm base with a 3 cm height.

Calculating the Area of a Circle and Drawing Circles

Notice the rubric calls for a circle of *approximately* 27 cm^2. This way we can round pi to 3 and make a radius of 3 cm for the proper area ($\pi \times r^2$ = area of circle). I had to teach the fourth and fifth graders how to draw a circle with a compass—as most of them had never used a compass before. We followed this with a mini-lesson about how to find the area of a circle. It was good teacherly fun at the beginning, however, when kids showed me a circle drawn freehand, and I said, "But that's not a circle! Here. Let me show you how to draw a perfect circle with a compass. Now, how do you draw a circle with the area of 27 cm^2?" All these minor issues turn into little puzzles and learning opportunities. Enjoy!

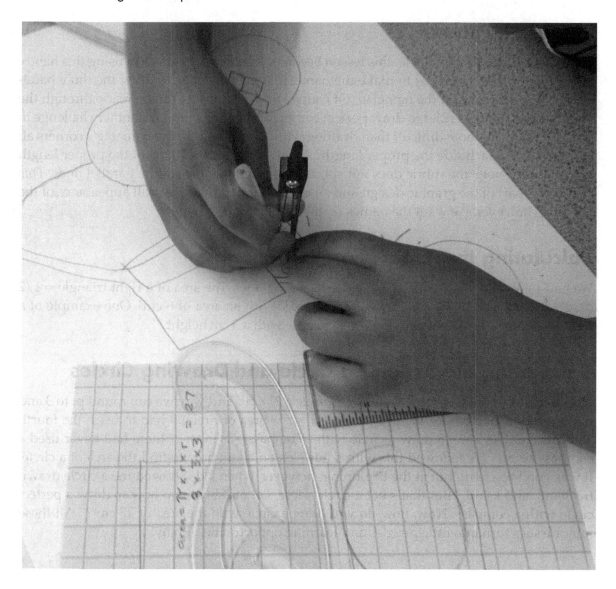

Drawing a Rhombus

Most of the students were unsure of what a rhombus looks like—confusing them with trapezoids or other shapes. For this lesson, we should use a rhombus which is easily separated into a rectangle and two right triangles. Use graph paper to practice drawing these before calculating area.

Area of a Rhombus

Choose a rhombus that can easily be separated into a rectangle and two right triangles. Using graph paper, show the students how to calculate the area of a rhombus—but be careful not to give them an answer which will equal 16 cm² so that they'll have to make that calculation themselves.

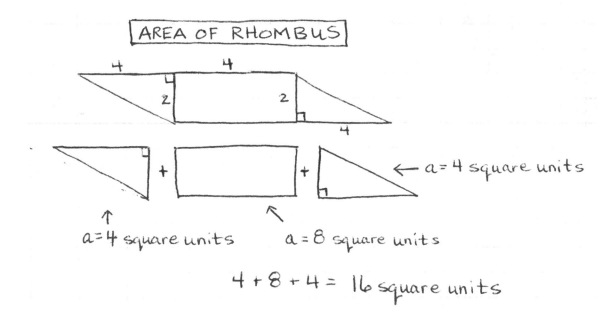

Excellent example of the design process for the rhombus. This student used graph paper to make a plan and then decided he could make an alligator from the rhombus.

So many times kids come up with ideas or methods I hadn't considered. Before beginning on a final product design, this student has made templates that he will use—making sure everything is the right size geometrically.

Desktop Nametag Design and Sales Project Guidelines

In this project you will design a nametag for a student's desktop. Your goal is to design an attractive nametag that will generate sales; however, you will need to keep the cost of producing the nametag in mind. The more the nametag costs to produce, the less profit you will make in selling the nametags. In addition, your nametags must fit the design requirements that follow. Consider your choices carefully. Your company wants the nametag to look great and generate volumes of sales, but it must fit the guidelines. Your teacher recommends making practice sketches and designs to begin.

- ◆ Each nametag must be a 25-cm × 8-cm rectangle with 90-degree angles on each corner. Measure and cut the nametag carefully from paper or cardstock.
- ◆ The design must include at least one of these three geometric shapes:

  - A circle with an area of approximately 27 cm^2
  - A rhombus with an area of 16 cm^2
  - A pair of right triangles, each with an area of 6 cm^2

- ◆ Use at least three colors, not including white.
- ◆ Include three parallel lines of 16 cm each where the student's name will be written.

Think, Plan, Sketch,

Design, Adjust . . .

Think Some More

Nametag Rubric

Advanced	Proficient	In Progress
• 25-cm × 8-cm nametag with perfect 90-degree corners	• 25-cm × 8-cm nametag with two or three corners at a perfect 90-degree angle	• Nametag is not 25 cm × 8 cm and fewer than two corners are 90-degree angles.
• Three parallel lines of 16 cm each make space to write a student's name.	• Three 16-cm lines create a space for a student's name to be written. They are not exactly parallel.	• Lines for the students' names are not present or not 16 cm in length.
• Includes rhombus of a 16 cm^2 area or two right triangles of 6 cm^2 each and a circle of approximately 27 cm^2	• Includes one or more of these three geometric shape requirements: a rhombus that does not meet the area requirements; two right triangles of 6 cm^2 each; a circle of approximately 27 cm^2	• The geometric shapes do not meet the area requirements or are not included.
• Required geometric shapes are a natural part of the design. It's not obvious they were included to fulfill a requirement for the assignment	• Required geometric shapes are placed in the design in a pleasing way. They do not detract from the overall effect of the nametag's design.	• The required geometric shapes seem to have been placed on the nametag as an afterthought to complete the assignment
• No calculation errors are made on the cost sheets, and the designer has a mathematical-logical explanation for why one company has been chosen over another company	• No calculation errors are made on the cost sheets. The designer has an explanation for why one company is preferred over another.	• One or more calculation errors are made on the cost sheets. No explanation is provided for why one company is preferred over another, or a cost sheet is completed for only one company.
• Exceptional graphic design qualities and features are noted below:	• Neatness and attention to precision in the graphic design. Some exceptional graphic design features are noted below:	• The nametag's graphic design appears to need another draft before it is transformed into a final product. Reasons noted below:

Name of Designer:

Copyrighted Logos (Optional)

Using a copyrighted logo adds a layer of understanding to the economics of this lesson as well as adding a 21st-century-technology graphic design challenge.

Discuss copyrights of logos with students and why a company needs to be protected by copyrights. Give the students an option of adding a copyrighted logo or trademark to their nametags for an additional "cost" of production (see the following chart).

If students want to add a logo, they'll need to find an image online and resize it appropriately for use with the nametag. Some of my students are pretty good at this already, and they tend to help others who struggle with the process.

Note: I have no idea what the actual cost of using a logo would be. The cost sheet is just for the purposes of this lesson—used to make an important economic point.

Discussion Questions

- What is a copyright?
- How does a copyright protect a company?
- What is "intellectual or artistic property"?
- Buying the rights to use a copyrighted logo can be costly. Why might it still be a good idea to purchase the right to use a logo?
- Why might a company choose not to sell the rights for their logo to be used?
- In some professional sports leagues, only one brand of clothing may be worn on the sidelines. If another brand is worn, the person wearing it is fined. Why?

Logos

You can expect trademarked or copyrighted logos to increase your sales, but will it be enough to cover the costs? Do you want to take the chance? Following are pricing guides for logos; however, you must write a letter to the company which owns a logo's trademark in order to gain permission to use the logo in your nametag design. Your teacher may add logos to the pricing guide when requests are made.

$50,000	$25,000	$10,000
Disney	Musicians or musical groups	Other logos not specified. Check with your teacher.
Nickelodeon	Restaurants	
Nike	Adidas, Reebok, and other sports companies	
Under Armor		
All Professional Sports Teams	College Sports	
	Older Movies	
Popular Video Games	Book Characters	
Apple and Microsoft	Older Video Games	
Popular Movies or Television	Other Cartoon Characters	
	National Clothing and Retail Chains	

Use the space below to write a letter to the company requesting permission to use their logo. Explain what you are using the logo for, and why you would like to use it.

Final Nametag Product

When students feel they have a draft ready for a final product, urge them to cross-check the rubric and then evaluate their own product based on the rubric.

Note: Students will not be able to complete the area of the rubric concerning the cost sheets and explanation for choosing one company over another. The teacher will complete this part of the rubric after the cost sheets are completed.

We design our final products on card stock. I have a few colors available, including white.

Students hand in the nametag along with their rubrics. I then add my evaluation to the rubric after students complete the cost estimate sheets ("It Makes Cents" handout).

For an added touch, laminate the nametags for a glossy finish.

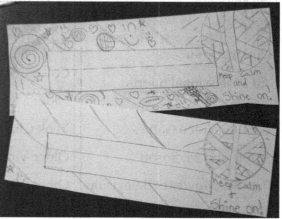
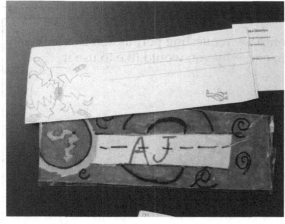
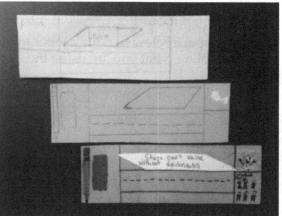

The images are of fifth graders' nametags in various stages of design. I like to see how they evolve through the process.

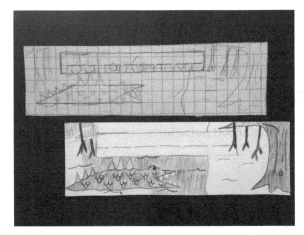

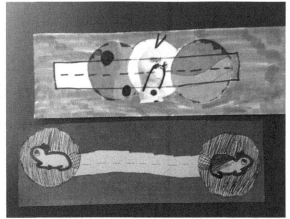

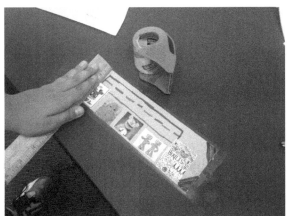

Some fifth-grade final products, including nametags that made use of a trademarked logo. "Tape lamination" on the left.

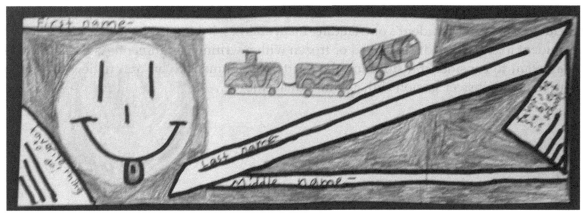

Lesson 5.2 Production Costs

In this lesson, students determine printing costs for 100,000 nametags.

Materials

- ◆ Handouts: "It Makes Cents," two per student
- ◆ Calculators (optional)

Estimated Time

30–60 minutes

Procedure

This lesson is right on target for a thorough understanding and application of place value and decimals. It's good practice for the older kids and includes multiplying decimals and determining a discount based on a percentage. My gifted mathematicians learned how to move the decimal to the right to multiply by 100,000 pretty quickly, and with help, they were able to calculate the discount.

Note: When I see that students have mastered a skill, I allow them to use a calculator. I also allow students to use a calculator to check their work.

This portion of the lesson also answers the question: "When will 1000th place value ever be important in real life?"

The following are the pricing guides for two different printing companies: Prairie Dog Discount Graphics and Graphix Incorporated. Determine print costs for 100,000 nametags for BOTH companies using two "It Makes Cents" accounting sheet handouts.

Note: It may be necessary to improvise a little bit on the color prices. These aren't the be-all and end-all of pricing sheets, but I tried to make them fairly inclusive and self-explanatory.

Once costs are determined, students will complete a short, constructed written response explaining why they've chosen one company over another. As this gifted programming includes a focus on a student's outstanding math abilities, it's important to consider whether a student may become disillusioned or frozen with a writing assignment. As a teacher, you may want to consider transforming the written assignment to an oral review or even a question-and-answer session with an individual student.

PRAIRIE DOG
DISCOUNT GRAPHICS
PRICING GUIDE
$20.00 PER 1,000 TAGS, 20,000 TAG MINIMUM

Primary Colors $0.0267 per Color
Blue
Red
Yellow
Black

Secondary Colors $0.0298 per Color

Green

Orange

Purple

Specialty Colors $0.0634 per Color

Pink, Sky Blue, Forest Green

Aqua, Cobalt, Silver, Rose, Gold, Lime, all others not listed.

Background Colors are Free!

Clip Art

$0.266

Trademarked Logos Pricing Available Upon Request

25% Discount on all Orders of 100,000 or More!

You Save!

We're Happy!

"Popping up to serve your large order printing needs."

Prairie Dog Graphics

Since 1977

Free Set-up on All Orders

Graphix Incorporated

Pricing Guide

.02 per Nametag—50,000 minimum order

Primary Colors $0.0175 per Color

Blue

Red

Yellow

Black

Secondary Colors $0.0266 per Color

Green

Orange

Purple

Specialty Colors $0.048 per Color

Pink, Sky Blue, Forest Green

Aqua, Cobalt, Silver, Rose, Gold, Lime, all others not listed.

Trademarked Logos Available

See Your Teacher for a Pricing Guide

Clip Art

$0.299

Background Colors

Primary—$0.065

Secondary—$0.081

Specialty—$0.097

$150 Set-up Fee on All Orders

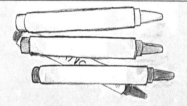

Name _____

Cost Estimate Worksheet for _____ (company name)

It Makes Cents!

Cost per tag (without printing) _____ x 100,000 = _____

Subtotal of Tag Costs

Print Colors

Color _____ Price _____ x 100,000 = _____

Color _____ Price _____ x 100,000 = _____

Color _____ Price _____ x 100,000 = _____

Color _____ Price _____ x 100,000 = _____

Color _____ Price _____ x 100,000 = _____

Subtotal of Print Colors Costs

Background Color

Color _____ Price _____ x 100,000 = _____

Subtotal of Background Color Costs

Set-up Fee

Price _____

Subtotal for Set-up Fee

Logo or Clip-Art Fee

Explanatory Note: _____   Price _____

Subtotal for Logo or Clip Art Fee

Discount

Change the Discount Percentage to a Decimal _____ x Total Cost Estimate _____ = _____ (Savings)

Subtract the Savings (answer above) from the Total Cost Estimate to Get the Actual Cost $ _____

Total Cost Estimate

Nametag Printing Company
Recommendation

Name_____

Explain which printing company you will use—*Graphix Incorporated* or *Prairie Dog Discount Graphics*. Use mathematical reasoning—including numbers and logic—to support the reason for your choice.

_____

_____

_____

_____

_____

_____

_____

_____

_____

_____

_____

Lesson 5.3 Determining Profit or Loss

This portion of the unit is the teacher evaluation component from which the students determine their profit or loss.

Materials

◆ Handout: "Profit-Loss Statement"

Estimated Time

20 minutes

Procedure

We award students net sales based on the scoring of their nametag rubrics. This process includes the production cost estimate that students completed when they chose a printing company in the previous lesson.

I recommend starting everyone with "breakeven" gross sales of nametags (unless the student needs to be taught some sort of lesson, but that's up to you). Beyond that, here is the scale I've used to determine profits:

◆ For every "Advanced Score" on a rubric item, add $5,250.00 profit.
◆ For every "Proficient Score" on a rubric item, add $2,725.00 profit.
◆ Add zero for "In Progress" scores.

I also recommend giving students back the money they've spent on any copyrights or trademarks. That's up to you as well. To me, this is not a lesson in advertising or marketing . . . and the kids have hopefully learned a bit about copyrights and trademarks already.

Gross Sales Example—See "Teacher Score Sheet"

Production/Printing Costs—$11,250.00
Copyright Cost—$25,000
Advanced Rubric Scores = 3 × 5,200.00 = $15,600.00
Proficient Rubric Scores = 2 × 2,725 = $5,450.00
In Progress Rubric Scores = 1 × 0 = 0
Total Gross Sales = $57,300.00
Total Net Sales = $57,300 − $36,250 = $21,050

Once again, duly noted . . . this is not a perfect system. All the actual numbers of printing costs and sales in the real world may be vastly different. That's not our point here. No matter what numbers we use (within reason), we have still learned important lessons in applied math and economics.

Once gross sales have been determined by scoring the rubric and completing the teacher records (see the following), students will complete the "Profit-Loss Statement" (also shown).

Nametag Teacher Score Sheet — Awarding Gross Sales

Student_____

Production/Printing Costs =   _____

Copyright Cost   =   _____

Advanced Rubric Scores = _____ x $5,200.00 =   _____

Proficient Rubric Scores = _____ x $2,725 =   _____

In Progress Rubric Scores = _____ x 0 =   ____0____

Total Gross Sales $

Teacher Records

Nametag Teacher Score Sheet — Awarding Gross Sales

Student_____

Production/Printing Costs =   _____

Copyright Cost   =   _____

Advanced Rubric Scores = _____ x $5,200.00 =   _____

Proficient Rubric Scores = _____ x $2,725 =   _____

In Progress Rubric Scores = _____ x 0 =   ____0____

Total Gross Sales $

Profit-Loss Statement

Name _____

Gross Income   ━━━━━━━▶ $ _____

Less Total Expenses

from "It Makes Sense" cost sheets   ━━━━▶ $ _____

Net Income   ━━━━━━━▶ $ _____

Gross Income Minus Total Expenses = Net Income

Lesson 5.4 (Optional) Tax Time

Once the profit, or gross sales, is determined, the project is complete. However, further challenges in calculating taxes (and another important economic lesson) might be the right choice for students who finish quickly.

Materials

♦ Handouts: "Income Tax Spending Categories" and "How Will My Income Taxes be Spent?"
♦ Calculators

Estimated Time

45–60 minutes

Procedure

Distribute the handouts. On the first handout, students calculate the amount of income tax they'll need to pay on their net profits.

In the second activity, students calculate how many of their tax dollars go to each area of government spending.

Finally, students think critically about how taxes are spent in a short, constructed written response. As with the written justification for printing company choices, weigh the practicality and purpose for a writing assignment at this point. Some students may be encouraged to discuss their choices with you instead of writing.

Round all calculations to the nearest penny.

Tax Time

James and James, CPAs

Good Day,

In response to your recent inquiry, we recommend that you make quarterly tax payments of 33% of your net income for the quarter. Here is how you'll calculate the amount of tax you owe:

- ◆ Multiply your net income by 0.33
- ◆ The product is the amount of tax you need to pay for the quarter

Log into your tax account online to pay promptly.

Total Tax to Pay Online _____

How Will My Income Taxes Be Spent?

Name_____

Each line below shows a category of spending for the U.S. government. Each category lists the percent of tax dollars that is spent for government programs in the category. Based on these percentages, how many dollars will you contribute to each category from your quarterly tax payment?

Source: 2013 Federal Taxpayer Return; www.whitehouse.gov/2013-receipt; percentages are rounded and may not total 100%.

National Defense (25%)   Amount You Contribute _____

Health Care (25%)   Amount You Contribute _____

Job/Family Security (19%)   Amount You Contribute _____

Education and Job Training (3%)   Amount You Contribute _____

Veterans Benefits (5%)   Amount You Contribute _____

Natural Resources, Energy, Environment (2%)   Amount You Contribute _____

International Affairs (2%)   Amount You Contribute _____

Science, Space, and Technology Programs (1%)   Amount You Contribute _____

Immigration, Law Enforcement, Administration   Amount You Contribute _____
of Justice (2%)

Agriculture (1%)   Amount You Contribute _____

Response to Natural Disasters (1%)   Amount You Contribute _____

Additional Government Programs (5%)   Amount You Contribute _____

Net Interest on National Debt (9%)   Amount You Contribute _____

Uncle Sam with boy and girl, from a WWI lithograph by James Montgomery Flagg, United States Library of Congress, circa 1918

Income Tax Spending
Categories

Name_____

Which is the most important category of spending for our tax dollars?
Explain why you've chosen this category, and explain what would happen if
spending in this category would either be increased or reduced.

_____

_____

_____

_____

_____

_____

_____

_____

_____

_____

_____

_____

Wrapping Up the Unit

Most students like to place their nametags on their desktops. They serve as a good conversation starter and as examples for others who may complete this project later.

Many of my students, when they have completed the project, like to design more nametags just for fun without the math calculations. We reserved an area on the wall for these additional nametags.

Sample Completed Project

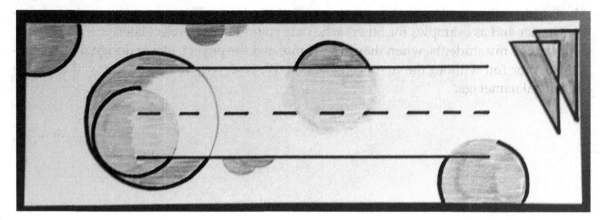

Nametag Rubric

Advanced	Proficient	In Progress
• 25 cm x 8 cm nametag with perfect 90 degree corners	• 25 cm x 8 cm nametag with two or three corners at a perfect 90 degree angle	• Nametag is not 25 cm x 8 cm and fewer than two corners are 90 degree angles
• Three parallel lines of 16 cm each make space to write a student's name.	• Three 16 cm lines create a space for a student's name to be written. They are not exactly parallel.	• Lines for the students' names are not present or not 16 cm in length.
• Includes rhombus of a 16 cm² area or two right triangles of 6 cm² each and a circle of approximately 27 cm²	• Includes one or more of these three geometric shape requirements: a rhombus that does not meet the area requirements; two right triangles of 6 cm² each; a circle of approximately 27 cm²	• The geometric shapes do not meet the area requirements or are not included
• Required geometric shapes are a natural part of the design. It's not obvious they were included to fulfill a requirement for the assignment	• Required geometric shapes are placed in the design in a pleasing way. They do not detract from the overall effect of the nametag's design	• The required geometric shapes seem to have been placed on the nametag as an afterthought to complete the assignment
• No calculation errors are made on the cost sheets, and the designer has a mathematical-logical explanation for why one company has been chosen over another company	• No calculation errors are made on the cost sheets. The designer has an explanation for why one company is preferred over another.	• One or more calculation errors are made on the cost sheets. No explanation is provided for why one company is preferred over another, or a cost sheet is completed for only one company.
• Exceptional graphic design qualities and features are noted below:	• Neatness and attention to precision in the graphic design. Some exceptional graphic design features are noted below:	• The nametag's graphic design appears to need another draft before it is transformed into a final product. Reasons noted below:
Very, very neat and exact. Wonderful use of colors—especially the blending in the circles.		

Welcome to 2nd Grade
Rapunzel

Designer's Name____SAMPLE_____

Name_____SAMPLE_____

It Makes Cents!

Cost Estimate Worksheet for __Graphix Inc.__
(company name)

Cost per tag (without printing) _.02_ x 100,000 = __$2,000_____

Subtotal of Tag Costs

$2,000.00

Print Colors

Color __purple__ Price ___.0266__ x 100,000 = _____2,660.00_____

Color __blue___ Price ___.0175__ x 100,000 = _____1,750.00_____

Color __sky blue_ Price __ .0480___ x 100,000 = ____4,800.00_____

Color _____ Price _____ x 100,000 = _____

Color _____ Price _____ x 100,000 = _____

Subtotal of Print Colors Costs

$9,210.00

Background Color

Color ___none____ Price _____ x 100,000 = _____

Subtotal of Background Color Costs

0

Set-up Fee

Price _____$150.00___

Subtotal for Set-up Fee

$150.00

Logo or Clip-Art Fee

Explanatory Note:_____ none_____   Price _____

Subtotal for Logo or Clip Art Fee

0

Discount

Change the Discount Percentage to a Decimal ___ x Total Cost Estimate ___ = _____ (Savings)

Subtract the Savings (answer above) from the Total Cost Estimate to Get the Actual Cost $_____

Total Cost Estimate

$11,360.00

Name_____SAMPLE_____

It Makes Cents!

Cost Estimate Worksheet for __Prairie Dog Discount Graphics__
(company name)

Cost per tag (without printing) _.02_ x 100,000 = __$2,000_____

Subtotal of Tag Costs

$2,000.00

Print Colors

Color __purple__ Price ___.0298__ x 100,000 = _____2,980.00_____

Color __blue___ Price ___.0267__ x 100,000 = _____2,670.00_____

Color __sky blue__Price __ .0634___ x 100,000 = ____6,340.00_____

Color _____ Price _____ x 100,000 = _____

Color _____ Price _____ x 100,000 = _____

Subtotal of Print Colors Costs

$11,990.00

Background Color

Color ___none____ Price _____ x 100,000 = _____

Subtotal of Background Color Costs

0

Set-up Fee

Price _____0___

Subtotal for Set-up Fee

0

Logo or Clip-Art Fee

Explanatory Note: _____none_____   Price _____

Subtotal for Logo or Clip Art Fee

0

Discount

Change the Discount Percentage to a Decimal _.25__ x Total Cost Estimate _13,990__ = 3,497.50 (Savings)

Subtract the Savings (answer above) from the Total Cost Estimate to Get the Actual Cost $__$10,492.50___

Total Cost Estimate

$13,990

Nametag Teacher Score Sheet — Awarding Gross Sales

Student_____SAMPLE_____

Production/Printing Costs =	_$10,492.50__
Copyright Cost =	___0____
Advanced Rubric Scores = __6_ x $5,200.00 =	_$31,200.00__
Proficient Rubric Scores = __0__ x $2,725 =	___0___
In Progress Rubric Scores = _____ x 0 =	___0___
Total Gross Sales	$ 41,692.50

Teacher Records

Nametag Teacher Score Sheet — Awarding Gross Sales

Student_____

Production/Printing Costs =	_____
Copyright Cost =	_____
Advanced Rubric Scores = _____ x $5,200.00 =	_____
Proficient Rubric Scores = _____ x $2,725 =	_____
In Progress Rubric Scores = _____ x 0 =	____0___
Total Gross Sales	$

Profit-Loss Statement for __SAMPLE_____

Gross Income $ 41,692.50

Total Expenses — from "It Makes Sense" cost sheets   — $ 10,492.50

Net Income   — $ 31,200.00

| Gross Income Minus Total Expenses = Net Income |

Profit-Loss Statement for _____

Gross Income $

Total Expenses — from "It Makes Sense" cost sheets   — $

Net Income   — $

| Gross Income Minus Total Expenses = Net Income |

Nametag Printing Company   Name____SAMPLE_____
Recommendation

Explain which printing company you will use—*Graphix Incorporated* or *Prairie Dog Discount Graphics*. Use mathematical reasoning—including numbers and logic—to support the reason for your choice.

It is much wiser for me to use *Prairie Dog Graphic Design*. I will save $867.00 if I use *Prairie Dog Graphic Design* instead of *Graphix Incorporated*. My savings come from the excellent 25% discount offered by *Prairie Dog Graphic Design*. If I did not have the discount, my order would have cost $13,990.00. With the discount, my order came to $10,492.50. Compare this to the total from *Graphix Incorporated* of $11,360.00. Since both companies offer very similar services, it is wiser to go with the least expensive choice so that I can maximize my profits.

Income Tax Spending Categories

Name_____

Which is the most important category of spending for our tax dollars?
Explain why you've chosen this category, and explain what would happen
if spending in this category would either be increased or reduced.

I believe that all of the areas are important. They all contribute to a strong nation. I wonder what would happen if education spending were increased? My older sister is just graduating from college, and she will owe $75,000 in student loans! She will pay the loans back because she is talented and responsible. I wonder, though, how many students will graduate and not be able to pay their loans back because of bad luck or irresponsibility? Maybe our country could help these students out. If we put more tax dollars into college tuition costs, we would have a stronger work force of young people. I think an increase in education spending will make students all the way down to pre-school better prepared. All good things will follow from this.

_____

_____

How Will My Income Taxes be Spent?

Name_____

Each line below shows a category of spending for the United States Government. Each category lists the percent of tax dollars that is spent for government programs in the category. Based on these percentages, how many dollars will you contribute to each category from your quarterly tax payment?

Source: 2013 Federal Taxpayer Return; www.whitehouse.gov/2013-receipt; percentages are rounded and may not total 100%

National Defense (25%)   Amount You Contribute $2,574.00_

Health Care (25%)   Amount You Contribute $2,574.00_

Job/Family Security (19%)   Amount You Contribute $1,956.24_

Education and Job Training (3%)   Amount You Contribute $308.88_

Veterans Benefits (5%)   Amount You Contribute $514.80_

Natural Resources, Energy, Environment (2%)   Amount You Contribute $205.92_

International Affairs (2%)   Amount You Contribute $205.92_

Science, Space, and Technology Programs (1%)   Amount You Contribute $102.96_

Immigration, Law Enforcement, Administration of Justice (2%)   Amount You Contribute $205.92_

Agriculture (1%)   Amount You Contribute $102.96_

Response to Natural Disasters (1%)   Amount You Contribute $102.96_

Additional Government Programs (5%)   Amount You Contribute $514.80_

Net Interest on National Debt (9%)   Amount You Contribute $926.64_

Uncle Sam with boy and girl, from a WWI lithograph by James Montgomery Flagg, United States Library of Congress, circa 1918

Scaling Skyscrapers

DOI: 10.4324/9781003257646-7

Background

Part one of Scaling Skyscrapers is an engineering challenge in which students build scale model skyscrapers using limited resources. Part two requires mathematical applications and logic as students apply math concepts to the scale.

In addition, this unit also contains the Skyscraper Cube Menu—a differentiated lesson built for students in six different learning styles. From math to language to research to design and acting, this menu is a big hit in my classroom.

Unit Objectives

The student will:

- ◆ Design and engineer a model skyscraper based on an actual building.
- ◆ Create a mathematical scale to compare a model skyscraper to its real counterpart.
- ◆ Understand mathematical comparisons and relationships as scale and ratios.
- ◆ Apply mathematical scale to complete an explanatory, creative writing task.

Math Common Core Standards

CCSS.Math.Content.5.NF.B.5 Interpret multiplication as scaling (resizing), by:

CCSS.Math.Content.5.NF.B.5a Comparing the size of a product to the size of one factor on the basis of the size of the other factor, without performing the indicated multiplication.

CCSS.Math.Content.6.RP.A.1 Understand the concept of a ratio and use ratio language to describe a ratio relationship between two quantities. *For example, "The ratio of wings to beaks in the birdhouse at the zoo was 2:1, because for every 2 wings there was 1 beak." "For every vote candidate A received, candidate C received nearly three votes."*

CCSS.Math.Content.6.RP.A.3 Use ratio and rate reasoning to solve real-world and mathematical problems, e.g., by reasoning about tables of equivalent ratios, tape diagrams, double number line diagrams, or equations.

Launch

Read aloud *The Man Who Walked Between the Towers*, a Caldecott Award–winning book by National Geographic Learning.

Allow students to share their impressions and reactions to this story in a class discussion. Furthermore, invite students to comment upon what qualities make the artwork in this book worthy of the Caldecott Award.

Finally, launch the Scaling Skyscrapers lesson by asking the students to speculate why many people are intrigued by skyscrapers. Answers will vary.

Lesson 6.1 Skyscraper Engineering Challenge

You might think of this lesson as the classic scaling activity—in reverse. In lesson 6.1, we start with an engaging engineering challenge without any mention of mathematical scale. That comes later. For now, it's all building fun . . . with purpose!

Materials

- ◆ Scissors
- ◆ Tape and/or glue
- ◆ Construction paper in a variety of colors with plenty of white, tan, and gray

Estimated Time

1 hour to 90 minutes

Procedure

I knew this was an engaging engineering and building activity when the first question was, "Do we get to take these home?"

Your students' nonverbal abilities and engineering skills will be challenged with this building activity, and they'll have to use problem-solving skills to work out construction problems and make a visual-mathematical connection. This engineering and construction challenge might seem easy to us as adults, but many of my fourth and fifth graders got that *far-off look* in their eyes as they scrunched up their foreheads and tried to figure out how they would make their skyscrapers take shape.

Project the photos of the four skyscrapers pictured to the entire class, search for the images online individually, or hand out paper copies to students.

Present the challenge to students in words similar to this script: *You must make a model of one of the four skyscrapers pictured—using only scissors, tape or glue, and construction paper. Don't tell anyone which skyscraper you are building. We want to see if you can make it look accurate enough for your classmates to recognize. You have one hour to complete the project.*

On the next page is the first of four photos of the four skyscrapers we use in my classroom. They are the Chrysler Building in New York City, the Smith Building in Seattle, the Flatiron Building in New York City, and the Willis Tower (aka Sears Tower) in Chicago. You might want to substitute a photo of a skyscraper from a nearby city instead. The photos are from the U.S. Library of Congress Prints and Photographs Collection where you may find many skyscraper photos in the public domain.

Source: www.loc.gov/pictures/item/2011634494/

Note that size, proportion, and scale are not part of the instructions. Allow students to build their models any size they'd like. In fact, the more sizes built, the more potential for understanding and discussion of scale in the next part of the lesson.

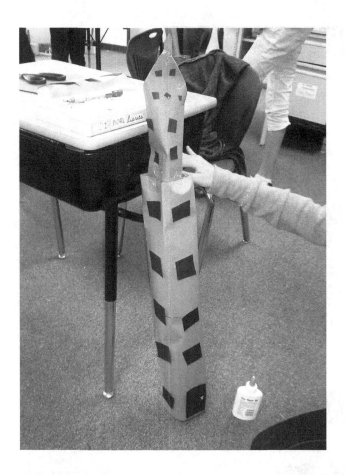

Lesson 6.2 Skyscraper Scale

After students challenge each other by trying to figure out which of the four models they've made, it's time to get out rulers and start a discussion of what scale is all about for lesson 6.2.

Materials

◆ Metric rulers or meter sticks
◆ Handout: "My Skyscraper Scale"

Estimated Time

20–30 minutes

Procedure

Students measure the height, in centimeters, of their model, and use this to complete the "My Skyscraper Scale" handout that follows. The handout does not contain all the necessary instructions to lead the students through the process of creating a scale, or mathematical relationship, between their model and an actual skyscraper. As a teacher, you'll need to lead students through the process described.

Instructions for the "My Skyscraper Scale" Handout

As my fourth and fifth graders are just beginners at simplifying mathematical relationships, we round measurements to the nearest 10s and 100s for our scale simplification process.

We'll use the familiar method of factor trees to simplify numbers and create a mathematical scale. This activity is an introduction to scale (which does not properly appear in most standards until seventh grade)—not a calculation challenge. Keeping our measurements in the 10s and 100s will help us visualize the real-life applications. Of course, if you are using this with older kids, you may prefer to use the actual numbers as an added calculation challenge. You might want to set up your relationship as a fraction or ratio instead. Our scale here is similar to a *scale of miles* on a map. The following are the approximate measurements of the skyscrapers pictured in this lesson:

◆ Chrysler Building, New York City: 320 meters
◆ Smith Tower, Seattle: 150 meters
◆ Willis Tower, Chicago: 525 meters
◆ Flatiron Building, New York City: 88 meters

The following is an example of how students will use factor trees to create a comparison scale between their model and the Chrysler Building.

First, measure the student's model in centimeters. In our example, the student's model measured 50 centimeters. Create a factor tree for the number 50.

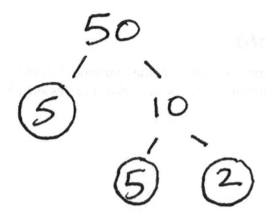

The factors are 5, 5, and 2 for this factor tree.

Let's say the student's model measured 53, not 50. Take a bit of a liberty here. The process of creating a mathematical scale through factor trees will not be very valuable using a prime number. Use 50 or 51 as a measurement instead.

Next, create a factor tree for the Chrysler Building's height of 320 meters. As advised earlier, I've taken liberties here for this activity. The true height of the Chrysler Building is rounded to 317 meters; however, 317 (a prime number with only two factors) is not a good number to work with for creating a simplified scale. The next step is to create a factor tree for the Chrysler Building, as follows.

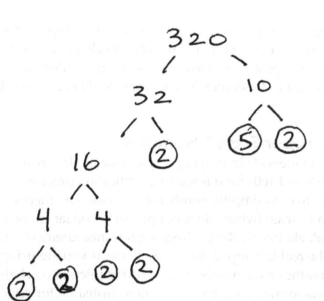

The factors are 2, 2, 2, 2, 2, 2, and 5.

If you have substituted local skyscrapers for the four examples I've used, round their heights to a number which will work well in a factor tree—unlike 317, for example.

The next step is for students to compare their model factor tree to the building's factor tree. Students will cross out equivalent factors shown in red.

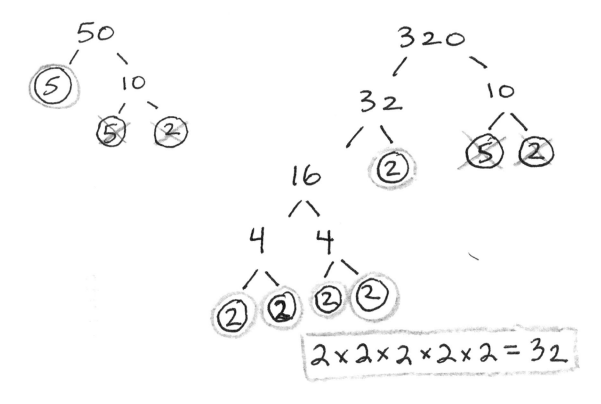

These factor trees share 5 and 2; we cross these factors out on the trees. The factor that remains in the model is 5. The factors remaining for the Chrysler Building are 2, 2, 2, 2, 2, which equal 32 ($2 \times 2 \times 2 \times 2 \times 2 = 32$).

We have thereby created a simple scale by calculating factor trees and comparing them. Our simplified scale is as follows:

5 centimeters for the model = 32 meters for the Chrysler Building or, as a ratio, 5 cm:32 m.

See the following "My Skyscraper Scale" handout example for this process using the handout.

My Skyscraper Scale

Name _____

A   Your Model Height in Centimeters Rounded to Nearest Ten =

_____

B   Actual Height of Skyscraper in Meters _____

Name of Skyscraper _____

Height A Factor Tree

Height B Factor Tree

Simplified Scale: Factor Tree A centimeters = Factor Tree B meters

Simplified Scale: _____ cm = _____ m

My Skyscraper Scale (sample)

Name_____

A	Your Model Height in Centimeters Rounded to Nearest Ten =
	__50 cm__

B	
	Actual Height of Skyscraper in Meters_____ __320__

Name of Skyscraper __Chrysler Building__

Cross out like terms between Factor Tree A and
Factor Tree B

Height A Factor Tree

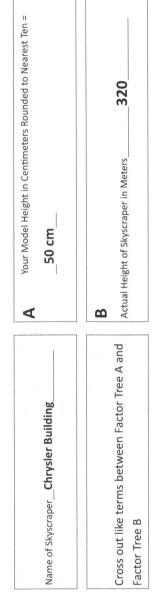

Height B Factor Tree

Simplified Scale: Factor Tree A centimeters = Factor Tree B meters

Simplified Scale: __5__ cm = __32__ m

Lesson 6.3 Discussion of Scale

We follow lesson 6.2 with a discussion about what our results show and fit the results into the language of the Mathematical Standards.

> CCSS.Math.Content.6.RP.A.1 Understand the concept of a ratio and use ratio language to describe a ratio relationship between two quantities. *For example, "The ratio of wings to beaks in the bird house at the zoo was 2:1, because for every 2 wings there was 1 beak." "For every vote candidate A received, candidate C received nearly three votes."*

Materials

◆ None

Estimated Time

15–25 minutes

Procedure

The following is a sample dialogue to start your discussion:

Let's look at the results you've found on your "My Skyscraper Scale" activity sheet. Your results might read something like 1 centimeter = 8 meters. What does this mean? (Allow time for responses and check for understanding.)

So for every 1 cm of height on your model, the real skyscraper is 8 meters high. If we look at just 3 centimeters on your model, then how many meters would this represent on the actual building? $3 \times 8 = 24$ meters

A scale is a relationship between two numbers. In mathematical language, we call this relationship a ratio. (Write the 1 centimeter = 8 meters scale on the board as a ratio: 1 cm:8 m.)

The ratio of centimeters to meters for my model skyscraper is 1 centimeter to 8 meters, or 1 cm:8 m, because for every 1 centimeter in height on my model, there is 8 meters in height on the real skyscraper.

On the back side of your "My Skyscraper Scale" handout, write your ratio in a way similar to the ratio I've written on the board. (Check for understanding.)

Let's try this out with some other examples:

◆ If the school is 7 meters high, and our ratio or scale is 1 cm:7 m, then how tall would a model of the school be? (1 cm)

◆ If Mount Everest is approximately 8,800 meters high, and our ratio is 1 cm:7 meters, then how tall would a model of Everest be? (1,257 cm)

- If you threw a "model" spitwad with the diameter of 7 cm at your teacher, and the ratio is 1 cm:15 m, then what is the diameter of the "real" spitwad? (105 meters!)

Can you think of examples of when *scale* is used? (architecture, any kind of model, toys, maps, etc.)

Why is scale useful? (Scale models are useful any time we need a "handy-sized" representation of something. Maps are a great example. It wouldn't do to have a map in its actual size, would it?)

Can you think of an example of a situation when it's useful to create a model scaled so that it is larger than the object it represents? (Anytime we need to examine small things, this sort of scale is useful. A doctor might use a large scale of a human ear for explanations to patients.)

Lesson 6.4 I Am a Giant

With this activity, students will apply mathematical scale to a more challenging level of depth of knowledge. In the related writing exercise, students make a visual–mathematical–language connection as they practice explaining by using logical thinking and details.

Materials

- ♦ Handout: "I Am a Giant"
- ♦ Meter sticks or measuring tape

Estimated Time

30 minutes

Procedure

Distribute the handout "I Am a Giant." The instructions are self-explanatory. Preview the instructions together with the students, and then support the completion of the activity as necessary.

Name_____

I am a Giant

With a partner, measure your height in centimeters.

I am _____ centimeters tall.

Take a few normal steps and have your partner help you measure the distance of your typical stride in centimeters.

My typical stride is _____ centimeters long.

Use this space to convert your height and stride length based on the following scale: 1 centimeter = 3 meters. What is your scaled height in feet, and what is your scaled stride length in feet? Make sure to show your calculations in the work space.

My scaled height = _____

My scaled stride = _____

Name_____

I am a Giant

With a partner, measure your height in centimeters.

I am _____152_____ centimeters tall.

Take a few normal steps and have your partner help you measure the distance of your typical stride in centimeters.

My typical stride is ____62____ centimeters long.

Use this space to convert your height and stride length based on the following scale: 1 centimeter = 3 meters. What is your scaled height in feet, and what is your scaled stride length in feet? Make sure to show your calculations in the work space.

152 x 3 meters = 456 meters tall

62 x 3 meters = 186 meters stride

My scaled height = 456 meters

My scaled stride = 186 meters

Giant Advantages and Problems

Name_____

Use the scale calculations you made on the *I am a Giant* activity sheet to answer this question: If you were a giant, what is one advantage and one disadvantage you would have with your new *scaled* size? Explain your answer using numbers from the activity sheet and from real life.

_____

_____

_____

_____

_____

_____

_____

_____

_____

_____

_____

Giant Advantages and Problems   Name _Sample_

Use the scale calculations you made on the *I am a Giant* activity sheet to answer this question: If you were a giant, what is one advantage and one disadvantage you would have with your new *scaled* size? Explain your answer using numbers from the activity sheet and from real life.

As a giant, I would enjoy advantages because of my size, but there would be disadvantages, too. One advantage is how easy it would be to walk to school. If each stride was 186 meters long, I could make it to school in one big leap. Once I got to school, being 456 meters tall, I would not even be able to sit inside the school building. I think I may need a book to read from that is about the size of a tennis court and pencil as long as an oak tree!

Supplementary Activities

The Skyscraper Cube

Often, students gifted in math do not need to review with the class before an upcoming test. There are times when students gifted in math have already mastered all of the content in an upcoming unit. These are two situations in which teachers may want to substitute the Skyscraper Cube for the content in the classroom.

> Why is the cube excellent for gifted learners?
>
> Because the 5 C's (Control, Choice, Challenge, Care, and Complexity) support gifted learners, and the cube addresses all five quite well.

1. Gifted learners need some CONTROL over what and how they learn. The cube offers six choices based on learning styles and adds variety to content. Importantly, the cube allows gifted learners to work at an accelerated pace or to slow down and go in depth, elaborate, and savor the details of a topic.
2. Gifted learners need some CHOICE in the topics in which they are engaged. The cube can be used to plan independent and personalized projects.
3. Teachers must CHALLENGE gifted learners with new material or in-depth studies. With a variety of categories and complex tasks, teachers can do just that.
4. Gifted learners must be given the chance to experience COMPLEXITY of content by moving past obvious relationships and making connections across disciplines.
5. Gifted learners need teachers who authentically CARE about gifted students. These teachers tend to have a profound impact on them . . . and if you offer the cube, you care.

Example dialogue: "We are working on a math review all week. I would love it if you guys can share some amazing thinking and math products instead of completing the review. Use this cube I made as a menu. Try to answer any questions you may have by collaborating along the way, but also know that I am here to help if you need it. We want you to share your products with the whole class two weeks from today."

Your group of gifted learners can individually tackle a portion of the cube's learning tasks, or they can choose just a few of the tasks to complete. They can collaborate on all or some of the cube tasks. Let the students decide as long as they are productive.

The first time you invite students to use a cube menu, it may take some extra coaching as you lay out expectations. For example:

1. Students are responsible for monitoring their own work and behavior.
2. Students have to decide how much work is acceptable (they will probably exceed this expectation).
3. Students may not draw attention to themselves. They need to try to solve issues on their own—academic, social, or otherwise, but they should expect help and guidance when necessary. Definitely never, ever brag about being in the cluster group!
4. Students are expected to share their products in some way.

What if the group or individuals in the group produce products inferior to the products of the rest of the class? They may need more coaching, and they need to understand that unproductive individuals will be *uninvited* to join the group in the future if the trend continues.

Important: This product should be ungraded. This doesn't mean feedback (focusing on the positive) can be skipped. It's quite possible many of your gifted learners are perfectionists, and they won't take chances or produce imaginative products and designs if a grade is a stake. Why risk it when you could simply do what the rest of the class is doing and slam dunk an A? Our purpose is to encourage kids to show their talents and follow passions. Our purpose is to help learners express their true potential by opening up and freeing up the academic context.

Important: This cube work should not be MORE work—just DIFFERENT work. There may be certain parts of the curriculum for which this group will need to be part of the regular class. That's fine. But do NOT make this a project students can do only AFTER they have done their regular classwork. This project is a substitute for other work—a more challenging substitute but not *more* in general.

Cube Menu Tool for Gifted and Talented
Skyscrapers

What are important ideas and designs that led to skyscrapers being built higher and higher?

Discover More

Build a model of an elevator. Bonus: Make it a working model.

Build or Create

How will skyscrapers look in the future? Share your ideas in any way you choose.

Imagine

Graph some of the world's tallest skyscrapers. Include another tall structure for comparison.

Calculate or Measure

Draw a detailed picture of a *cornice* you've found on an old building. Design your own cornice, too.

Draw or Design

Write or tell us about a famous skyscraper story.

Perform or Write

Bonus Challenge

Create a geometrical NET for a skyscraper. Create a city street!

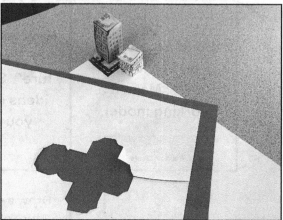

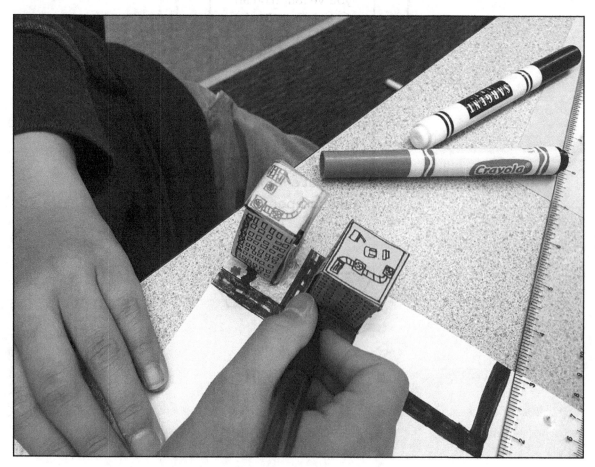